THE JOY OF A TRUE FIGHTER

GOD'S TRANSFORMING POWER
DIRECTLY FROM PRISON

BY MICHAEL A. LEWIS

© 2007

By Michael A. Lewis

All Rights Reserved

PaperWood Publishers

ISBN: 978-0615993386

All Scriptures quoted are from
The King James Version of the Bible

Contents

Introduction	11
Inspired by Struggle	15
Some that Seek a Heavenly Cure	21
Witnessing His Power	27
An Experience of God's Presence as You Struggle	31
An Anointing that Motivates	37
Behold a True Fighter	49
Battered in the Ring	57
Don't Neglect Your Station	75
A King in Rebellion	85
A Gift in a Humble Fighter	91
Why a Wilderness Experience is Necessary	103
Face the Enemy Head On	113
Using a Lie as a Lethal Weapon	117
Suffering for Righteousness	129
The Devil Will Give the Idle Work to Do	135
The Example of Struggles	149
Protecting Your Vitality	163
Employing a Winner's Attitude	177
A Power Within Reach	195
A 30 Day Devotional	201

Acknowledgments

This book is written to point out to the world that the power of God is without limitation. God's power and His Spirit transcends boundaries, He manifests Himself behind prison walls. My desire is that the world would know that God is still reaching the unreachable. He's still reaching out to the rejects, the outcast, and the disenfranchised with a love beyond human comprehension.

It still baffles me that God would consider saving someone such as me. I am truly a great witness of His power to transform lives. You will find in these pages topics of how to live victorious over sin. How to resist the Tempter. How to fight through your struggles and win, more importantly. By the saving power of the cross, the precious blood of Jesus Christ which provides salvation.

As I continue growing in Christ, I become more convinced that the Spirit of God wanted me to write this book to share with all the mighty and awesome things which the Lord is doing, what He can do and what He continues doing. It's my motivation to write this book as a testament of God's unfailing love.

Many thanks to my Chaplain and Pastor, Rev. Dr. Gideon Jebamani who gave me the opportunity to lead and to share my gifts and talents with the body of Christ, and to Pastor Duval and his team. I really appreciate your love and thoughtfulness. Thanks to Mr. Terry Presley who volunteered his services, making corrections and tolerating my constant nagging. Mr. Anthony Dixon, I may never be able to put into words what your many gifts, love and encouragement mean to me. You are truly a great blessing. Elder Edwards Johnson, you are a shoulder to lean on especially when times are tough, you keep saying, "keep going man, you'll make it!" On the real, thanks to all my brothers in Praise Unlimited, especially to the Music Director, Bro. Will. Such an outstanding choir, I cherish your gifts, talents and great Christian support, loving it when you uplift my spirit in songs. I can never forget my friend and brother, Paul Clark and his wife Sheila, who have been standing with me from day one! You both are truly inspiring. I still can never forget the many kind of words of my brother, my mother's son, Pastor George Brown, a great man of God: "walk in the way, seek and ask for the old path, where is the good way." Thanks to my brother John and Doc, my wonderful sister Petol, you are truly a very inspiring sister for real. All my wonderful children, Lanique, (Baby Girl) Tevin (Little T) and Demani (King D). I love you all so very much, what could life really be without you? To all my beloved friends, loved ones and my fellow compadre, thanks for your support and prayers. I love you, I need you and you are truly appreciated. This is my first writing and somehow I just pray something here will touch someone's life. God bless!

This book is dedicated to:

My three angels, such wonderful children, Lanique (Baby Girl), Demani (King D), Tevin (Little T). You are indeed my greatest motivation. God uses all of you as an inspiration. I find strength to carry on because of you.

Introduction

Oh, the many wonders that are wrought through struggles! Struggle is a wonderful birthplace where we can appreciate life to the fullest. And it is when you begin to view things from a different perspective. One must understand the overall necessity for it. Then the approach which is employed to deal with them will have greater meaning for years to come. Many people, to a 'great extent, have taken life for granted not realizing how precious this wonderful treasure is. Every single day we are to live the best we can as if it's our last day. Broadly speaking, however, it takes one with courage and tenacity to realize that there is deep and important essence of going through a cycle, yet not knowing how you'll make it but, owning that courage which had been impregnated somewhere on the inside, and, since you are convinced of life's vicissitude, knowing that labor is imminent, one day finally, the load you carry, there is hope of a perfect delivery.

The fact that trouble does not last forever, though weeping may endure for night, joy certainly will come in the morning! The night, though it may seem long. Since you've made it to this present journey of midnight, you have only just a few more turns and twisting, then dawn will break forth and sun will come out beyond your horizon. Gladly will I toil and suffer, even as the pains and pangs increases, there's yet an unspeakable joy bursting like flames on the inside. You are possessed with that steadfast hope that the sun will come out tomorrow!

Have you ever seen a forty eight hour night? No! That's not possible, night follows day and after winter, there will be spring, and buds will be blooming. Don't you know you're getting ready to blossom again? Then stop worrying yourself to death! Don't feel pressured believing that just because your leaves have fallen, you are dead and decomposed. Nature's process must prevail so that in time your beauty and texture can be displayed. Struggles are the most precious ointment to texturize your beauty. That's a beauty that glows, a beauty which is appreciated to the eyes. It is true that one will laugh out loudly, gazing with admiration once you complete the journey through your long and winding tunnel. It is what God will do, the perfect author and finisher of your faith. Your struggles are not meant to distort your beauty. Do you seriously believe that a mother with child is cursed because she struggles? Through this is a natural process, there's an ongoing struggle, yet at labor, the floods of joy, the many kisses to the young. God made struggles to bring out perfection!

Have you ever seen a bunch of rose in the month of June? That's an ideal beauty to cherish. Yet, just a few months ago, those same plants were just as dead. Haven't you got some courage just to wait until June so you can bloom again? The rain did not kill you, neither did the snow. Through many blizzards, twisters and floods you are still here! June is right around the corner, the winter is gone, hold on! Press on! You are not alone, "lo, I am with you alway,"[1] saith the Lord. Not even you won't believe how very beautiful you'll be in June, yet, because I've known it, I've

---

[1] Matthew 28.20

proven it and I am telling you, just hold on! The air will be fresh again then at last you'll smile at the joys of your overcoming victory. Your skies will all be blue forever, it's a hope that will never end, a hope in God, through Jesus Christ.

Inspired by Struggle

Chapter One

A man once told me, he's been smoking since he was twelve years old, now at forty-six, he was ready to quit. I have one pack and some, once those are finish, that's it! I won't ever smoke again, he said. It is strange that in life, even when we're getting older, our sad games are never over, we still have the tendency to lie, even to ourselves. If you really want to quit smoking, just quit! Throw them in the garbage, that's it! If you'll have to wait until you finish what you have, then quit, that will never happen because by the time you got through with those, you'll get the urge again for more and the truth is, those urges will be much stronger, they'll never go away.

Another young man said, "I'll never cheat on my wife ever again!" That's a very bold statement. It's very good to entertain those feelings, however, it was later revealed that this same man was still in possession of his mistress apartment keys, and in the trunk of his car was important belongings that was never turned over to her. When you make a conscious decision to turning your life around, there's got to be important actions which follows. You must relieve yourself of some stuff! You must do some house cleaning and anything that will cause you to stumble must be carefully expunged.

When Jesus came to Zacchaeus with the gift of salvation, his desire was to be faultless, he was ready to clean his house of every corrosion. Zacchaeus was completely determine to give back anything he thought he had acquired by false pretense. Don't ever put off for tomorrow what is only right for you to do today, delay is still danger! Jesus calls his disciples to follow him, yet some wanted to take care of some unfinished business. Suffer me to go and bury my father. Jesus said, follow me, and let the dead bury their dead. When you come to Christ, all other obligations are to be second place to the master. When the master said, "come with me," it's not even necessary to go and bid farewell. Following Christ is of paramount importance and must hold prominence over anything else regardless of its value. There's no struggle that can or should confront us that even in our weakness forces us to putting down our cross or denying our savior. When you're confident in the God that holds the weight of this world in his hands. To be clear, the greater your pains are, it's undeniable the more weightier your cross, the more longer your bridge is, I say, as you proceed forth through burning and bleeding because of the many pressures in the constricting journey, you are never alone, but sharing in the experiences of your Lord and at last, as you reach the threshold of your destination, behold, eyes hath not seen, neither ear heard, neither have entered into the heart of man, the things which God hath prepared for them that love him.

You must be able to view a far off from your destiny what is ahead in the spirit. Having that spirit's view, it will be a motivational factor, just like Jesus who saw from a distant the salvation of souls and how through his suffering millions will be rescued from the pit of hell. Christ carried the cross though bloody and painful, and he endured. But for the joy that was set before him, he endured the cross, despising the shame and is sitting at the right hand of God. Something must be seen or felt in you, in your spirit, just like a pregnant mother, she felt that kicking inside her womb, yet, it could kick till Jesus comes, for her, it was a pleasure, because in her pains she was viewing a beautiful baby and oh, the sweet joy when she places her eyes on that precious thing she carried. She wishes she could do it over again. In your struggles you must feel the kicking and refuse to buckle under the pressures of life but see the many wonders of God's miracle working power, as you push and push during your labor.

Paul the apostle was out there in the raging sea trying to make it to the shores, out in the middle of the gigantic ocean, though his mind was fixed on land, here he suffers a great shipwreck. This was no doubt a heart wrenching and devastating crisis. Regardless of one's faith in God, there comes a time when a severe crisis will silently come to shake your faith. At sea, it was cold and black, and night was even longer than usual. A severe faith test is never a sweet one, once you think that you've now getting to the final aspect of your journey, coming closer to land, you find that the enemy had already set up another ferocious wind that pulls you back under. This is when you find that if your faith is not truly anchored in a foundation deep, you will certainly be bankrupted into the ocean swells. What a man of faith Paul was, he relaxed, finding strength in his God, the God that was able to pull him through. On that ship, his confidence had never wavered, he was trusting in the God that had revealed himself to him on the road to Damascus.

It's easy in life's struggle to cop an easy way out, well, since it get to this, in your frustration, I'll just abandon the ship. I might just have to leave everyone else for dead. Yes you can be out there feeling weary and done, maybe thinking that the fishes will have a good time but, only when God refuses to act then you might as well become hopeless. I tell you this though, the Almighty God will never, has never cease to act on the behalf of his children. Just at the worst place that you may have found yourself, even buried underneath the waves, you can never stop trusting , because I have heard of a Jesus who speaks to the wind, he speaks to the sea, and the wind and the waves obeyed his voice! Yes Jesus still speaks to a raging sea and at his direct command, the mighty wind and the powerful waves obeyed his voice. Jesus don't even have to shout, he never preached, he never used any force, Jesus silently breath from his mouth "Peace" and oh how well a word from the Master's lips will change even the forces of nature.

To be inspired by struggles, it might not be the most popular thing for popular people. Don't you ever tell popular folks to trust in God when problems seem like they'll never end. Popular folks seek medication, they seek therapeutic intervention. Popular folks needs drugs and yes they'll drink themselves into a frenzy not realizing that their problems will remain even after all those efforts. Why is it so unpopular in today's world to take the God of the universe at his word when you face life's upheavals? I know that Jesus has never lost a battle, he has never failed even in the most daunting times. People need to turn to the cross of Calvary and in their pains just call on the Lord Jesus who is sufficient in times of need. To the natural man that's just foolishness, in an educated world, they in their intellectual ability will only seek advice from their sophisticated colloquies, who's wisdom are only engraved in their degree, yet, I know that a degree will not be as powerful as the degree of Prayer, because I know that prayer can still move mountains. If they would just come down from their high, and would now lower themselves on bending knees and storm the gates of heaven, then they would began to experience a rising tide of peace in their insurmountable struggles.

Even now, it is true that only God is ever able to speak into a troubled soul where that soul will unload his burden with blood, blood that was spilled at Calvary, which will never loses its power. A medicated society, with a medication for every burden, yet, if we can only reject them and receive the medicine from the balm in Gilead, how much by the millions would be healed.

Some That Seek
A Heavenly Cure

৪০

Chapter Two

The bible speaks of one very courageous woman that was struggling. This sister was desperate and had exhausted all remedies seeking a cure for her ailment. It is very fascinating that there are those women that under extreme pressure will put their life on the line seeking for something that is very precious to them. What will you risk to receive your healing? This woman was constantly bleeding and for twelve years one could just imagine the disgustingness of her condition. A woman told me that bleeding is her only regret been a woman and that she just can't stand it at all, not even for a day. She went on to say, I only cope with that part of been a whole woman. Well, this very rare condition which was plaguing this one sister, and in her plight, she heard of a man that got a real remedy, whose power to heal was never a fairy tale. She in her struggle was inspired by obtaining the well needed information about Jesus. "Lord I have adjusted to an eight day cycle which was very difficult and now here am I at this moment dealing with this issue for twelve years, God it is tough!" I've had enough! In your pains and struggles, you must get to the place where you become really tired. The sister was so very "sick and tired of been sick and tired," to the extent that she left her home ahead of time only after hearing that the Master was coming to town. She was totally determined not to miss out on the one opportunity to be healed, she positioned herself.

Why or how could you harbor hate towards a woman of courage? A desperate woman will team the craft to getting in position. When you want to live, when you know the sweetness of life and is convinced that God is not through with you yet, somehow though, life seem to be giving you a raw deal. Remember that The Lord Jesus is passing by your way! Whatever it takes for you to get back in line, it's important that you position yourself! You just can't sit there and cry, don't give up on life, don't just sit in your condition believing the lies of Satan. He wants you to think that it was a part of God's plan for you to be diseased, he wants you to think it was your destiny so just remain in that state. Get up! Get out of the bed, get out from your easy chair and go down to that place, a place where the Lord Jesus is about to pass.

Now, "He that dwelleth in the secret place of the most High shall abide under the shadow of the Almighty."[2] I will say of the Lord, he is my refuge and fortress, in him will I trust. It's time for those that are sick, those who are hurting, to gather up some courage, arm yourself in the faith and go get the cure that you need. Jesus is passing by your way! Today! Your healing is available, it's still in the blood! Your sister did not allow doubts to take her under, in the crowd she pressed and by faith was only able to touch the hem of

---

[2] Psalm 91.1

Christ garment and that was all she needed. Just one faith touch of the Master's clothing! Why sit there and die? To be inspired by struggle is to press, taking the less popular direction. Inspired means to be motivated even in pains! It means to cultivate a joy under the most adverse circumstances and acting as though things are normal anyhow. It is to employing the notion and self-will, that when the going gets tough, the tough gets going! I shall not die but live to declare his goodness. The God of Heaven is so much greater than the struggles of life, he don't have to speak to get the job done, all you have to do is touch him, don't hug on him, don't shake his hand, don't kiss him, just touch the tail of his garment! There is a healing virtue even in the tail of his garment.

Have you ever stopped and wondered why in your struggles there are folks who harbor a ridiculous notion that just because you are overtaken by a severe storm, like it will completely sweep you away? Sadly they began to rejoice because to them, you'll be a goner. To those folks they need to realize that some storms are never always a worst case scenario for a saint of God. When they thought there will never be a tomorrow, God will send a whale, a friendly whale, one that is only coming to your rescue.

I have seen in the Apostle Paul's discourse, after his worst experience at sea. Yes, Paul was walking with the Lord, his life was already changed by the power of God and although walking with God he endured some great faith test. We must never come to a place in our lives, walking with a chip on our shoulders and began to feel that just because you are walking with God you are immune from crushes and attacks from the enemy. Paul was very accustomed to various attacks and yes, there are those that will see a child of God in his struggle and would stand by delighting in his pains, speaking evil against him, even praying that his problem would continue to plague him.

You see some storms are not from the enemies, God will put you to a place just with the intention of showing you what folks really thought about you. Some of the people that you had thought were actually your friends were your worst enemies. Oh, they began to make all kinds of comments, "Those things are happening to him because he's not really saved, oh he's guilty of such and such, oh he's living in sin, that's why he lost his home." Paul after finally making it to land was now on the island called Melita, the people of Melita welcomed him and took care of him, making sure that he was warm. While Paul was gathering sticks, and laid them on the fire, suddenly a viper came up out of the heat and fastened on Paul's hand. Now the people saw what had happened and began to look on Paul now not as a man of God, but as a murderer. In your life you see, unfortunate situations happened one behind the other. Then the people around you having a changed prospective regarding who you really were. You've done all the good you can, have been abused many times all for your love and kindness, yet due to the faith you have in God, you will remain firm not allowing the skeptics to cause you to lose your grounds.

You can, like Paul, shake off the beast into the fire and the Bible said, he felt no harm! The truth of the matter is, many people that don't love you are standing around waiting for you to fail, they might be even praying for the day that you fail, so that they can laugh and have a party. But once they realize that you have endure the beatings, the whipping and the many tortures, they even hate you the more. They want you dead, my friends! When the snake bit Paul, it was something that they thought would make them celebrate. When you go through your pains, they won't console you, they won't visit you, and they won't support or lend you a hand. They want to make sure that you stay down! Have you ever wonder why some people are so surprise that you are still standing after all you've been through? You can see the expressions, some say you've got nine lives, but it's not true, you're been sustained by the power of God! Never mind the folks that would dare come in contact while you were there in the dirt. They are now ready to join you. They saw how you are making it, an overcomer, now they want to join you to find out your secret.

Let them know that it is God! The God of Abraham and Isaac and Jacob! When those enemies that had wanted the worst for you see you standing by the glory of God, they will have a change of heart and come to know that the Lord Jesus Christ is the reason for your hope. Be it known unto you all, and to all the people of Israel, that by the name of Jesus Christ of Nazareth, whom ye crucified, whom God raised from the dead, even by him doth this man stand here before you whole. This is the stone which was set at naught of you builders, which is become the head of the corner. Neither is there salvation in any other, for there's no name given among men whereby we must be save. You will make it without a doubt, just because of Jesus!

Suddenly, they saw the Paul that they would have thought to be dead, standing after knowing the histories of those poisonous snakes, he was completely immune to their venom and what they witnessed, they couldn't help it but call the man of God, "god!" If you face your snake bites with courage, you will soon realize that you will be looked on with respect and dignity. Even your enemies will see you in admiration and will one day call on you to their rescue when they are faced with life's challenges. Yes, going through your pains should motivate you to learn the art of prayer so that when you stand to pray for those that hates you, they will experience the power of healing and will in turn gained that assurance that you are truly a man of God. Courageous Christians cannot afford to fold and grow weary in the painful experiences that you face. A great witness for Jesus is to stand in the face of evil, facing head on the enemies, been bold in the faith that you have in the Lord, then those that harbor doubts, will come to accept because of the living witness in which you proclaim.

Witnessing His Power

※

Chapter Three

The more I sit and reason about Jesus, I am more convinced of the reassuring hope which inspired the saints of old. I believe that the road to Calvary had not been easy, carrying the cross had not be easy, even the agonizing pains, been brutally whipped. Yet, as I consider from a distant the ultimate gain, I cannot help but to fall down on my knees in complete penitence before a great God to grant me more strength and more courage to even be bolder to stand up for him. If what he suffers for me, I can have the courage to even go the limit, not harboring doubts, then that's a small price in comparison to what the Lord has done.

What motivated Christ to complete his earthly mission for our victory? It was his ability to pray in season and out of season, Christ was very instant in prayer. The Lord Jesus was ever constant in communication with the Father and the Father had never cease to out pour that supernatural anointing so that even when Christ would pray, Father, if it be possible, take this cup, yet, if not my will, let thy will be done. Having confidence that he was never alone, because the Father floods him with that will to persevere.

In the blackness of your pains, you must remember that you are never alone. After coming to the place of acknowledging the ever presence of his exceeding glory, it should be a driving force that your darkness will not always be dark, the sun will certainly come out tomorrow! The Son never ceases to shine even though you in your dark tunnels refuses to see the light. No matter how it may seem, the wonderful Son is ever shining! If you will only believe in your heart that God's Son, the beloved Savior, is still shining brightly even in your dark tunnel.

As a secure victory for you, you must be able to see the living Christ going the distant with you. It pays to understand that as a child of God, heaven will never forsake you because of the raging sea experience. A major fire is no deterrent for a God that conquers hell. Even in the fire, your God has the capacity to just appear! God will not refuse to walk faithfully, hand in hand with his children. It matters not if his children will rebel, trying to flee from his assignments, God will join you in your boat to Tarshish and if you harbor any doubts whether he'll see you or not, you will soon realize that a great whale will soon swallow you into safety. The motivating factor with God is that you can never hide from his presence. Neither in mind, body or spirit can you hide from God because even your thoughts he is acquainted with. David said it best, "Whither shall I go from thy spirit? Or whither shall I flee from thy presence? If I ascend up into heaven, thou art there: if I make my bed in hell, behold, thou art there. If I take the wings of the morning, and dwell in the uttermost parts of the sea; even there shall Thy hand lead me, and thy right hand shall hold me."³ The gracious eyes of the Lord is still running to and fro the earth and it's impossible for us to ever escape him. God looks down even on the sparrows, his eyes behold them.

To be inspired in my struggles even goes deeper because the God of creation cares so much for me at the most crucial moments. I obtain a reassuring confidence of his ability to provide for me. My needs will be met because the God in whom my faith rested knows already of all that is needed for the day. He is still the greatest need supplier, I will wait patiently on him. Is God capable of distributing necessities? He expresses a keen interest in the lilies of the field, how they are beautifully dressed, even the sparrows, he fed them. Don't you know that you are a child of The Most High God? If he then could carefully meet the needs of lilies, sparrows and all his creation here on earth, then how about you? Are you not seriously greater to him than all those things?

You and I were wonderfully created in God's divine image and you and I are too special to God, he would never refuse to keep his promise. It is true that our struggles are necessary so that God's plans and purposes can be fulfilled which is a motivation for us to press forward. Well if I'm more special to God, why do I have to struggle? Well, are you more special than his beloved son Jesus? Well, his only begotten son suffers and his suffering was to the point of death, a penalty paid for you and me! Well, don't you know that since he struggles, you likewise must encounter some share of his experience?

---

[3] Ps 139:7-10

What do you think it was like for Jesus? Well, for he hath made him to be sin for us, who knew no sin; that he might be made the righteousness of God in him. There is a penalty for sin, oh yes, the wages of sin is death and by a consequence of our sins Jesus, took your place. Let me tell you, he have paid a huge price, it was hard! Go-d's son left his home in glory coming to earth to be a "Scape Goat" for us. If Christ refuses his own comfort in heaven, coming to die on earth, then you and I are to at times relinquish our own comforts, dying to self and to be alive to righteousness. It is very vital for life's existence. Christ is very much attracted to pain. He himself felt what pain was about, still he provided a way out for you, taking your pains on himself because on that bloody cross, Jesus took not only our sins but our sickness and decease, trust me he was wounded for our transgressions too!

The Lord was bruised for our iniquity and the chastisement of our peace was upon him and by his stripes we are healed, glory to God! It is true that the man that knows God will not refuse to trust him because of his ongoing struggles. God provides every opportunity for change even sending his son to suffer in our place.

An Experience of God's Presence as You Struggle

Chapter Four

    Beloved, your future will ultimately be better than your past. Just never say that your best days are behind you when the Lord has promised you a future of hope. This hope which hinges on faith that God is the one to determine the very outcome of your future. The very fact that God will give you this future means that it will be a secure one. A person whose hope is in God needs not to fear but in the most pressing moments feel God's presence and know with all assurance that the hands of God are on your life. Many times you'll feel that pulling in your belly that something good is about to break. You must be able to smell the sweet aroma of the "alabaster box" of your life and inhale it's freshness, just basking in the glory of the wonderful fragrance of your blessing. Many times God will send a reassuring push that will be a sign that his hands are still on your life and that all you'll have to do is wait, just take a nice sniff of what's to come and wait!

When the bible speaks of seasons, it should never be underestimated because, God does have a time when he'll just show up with favor from on high. A great season of harvest is about to break forth on your behalf and you'll wonder in amazement after viewing the awesomeness of God's power. God will recompense you for your patience, he'll give you double for your trouble, moving in your life with what you'd call "A shower!" It's raining down from the throne of God. An outpouring rain, showers of blessings, oh that today they might fall, grant to us now a refreshing, come now and honor thy word! It is a great reward to remain faithful, it's true that a man that will remain unshakable in his great storms of life will never be ignored by the God of heaven. God is actively looking down on him with great plan to one day flood him with a bounty of blessing. Times and seasons are equally important with God, the drought is only for a season, likewise a storm is for a season but at spring time, you began to see the flowers blooming.

Many of us will not enjoy a "catch crop" blessing, the short season that produces tomatoes and peas is never that same season for coconuts. Yes, coconuts takes much longer, you'll have to wait and wait to enjoy this produce, yet it's what produces the best tasting oil, this oil is what represents the anointing! "Thou anointest my head with oil, my cup runneth over![4] Anointing takes toiling, patience and struggle. The taller you'll climb it takes more anointing just like a tall coconut tree which produces the best oil. It is true that just when the coconut is ready, you still must wait some more for it to dry, it takes courage and endurance that's why obtaining this anointing you are endeavor to cherish it. An anointing that never pass through fire will not hold

---
[4] Psalm 23.5

endurance. It is the fire, that constant burning is what mold, shape and conform. God works powerfully in the anointing that burns and the more the burning is the more stronger the testimony of God's miracle working power, because you will shine and out last others as you stand as a representative of God's greatness.

When the word of God spoke to the prophet Jeremiah to go to the potter's house, it was a powerful revelation that at this house, God is really at work. What is actually going on at the potter's house? A constant burning! If you're really seeking a double portion of God's power, you must be prepared to go on the wheel. You just cannot be afraid of the burning heat, on God's wheel, there is an intense heat and if you are a constant complainer, murmuring about the temperature, you won't get it because all that you will need is in the heat! People don't understand the nature of certain vessels, you cannot put any kind of vessel on the heat. It's got to be made right!

That vessel must be made out of the best materials that will withstand very high velocity of heat. When God choose you to be the right vessel, he knows that you've been made with the right material, when the heat began its penetration, you will withstand! You've seen how very easily some vessels dissolve? So easily they crumples and become useless, it's because of the condition of their material. Watch for its structural design and durability. I've seen many wonderful saints that we've thought were filled with the Holy Ghost and fire, yet were placed under test and couldn't stand. It's not all the saints that proclaimed to be possessed with durability are actually durable, that's why the Lord went further and states, "an infilling with the Holy Ghost and fire!"

It doesn't just stop at the Holy Ghost, the fire is so essential! It's something special about the fire, what you'll never purchase like some charcoal at the Walmart stores. The bible said, tarry here until you are endowed with power from on high! It's not a quick take out, drive through, express or an "EZ" pass experience, you must tarry, exercising patience. You got to wonder sometimes, where do some folks get their Holy Ghost? Every word spoken by them, you'd hear them speaking in unknown tongues that sounds really good, yet there's no structural design, no durability because all they've gotten is tongues without fire! That's why until God places you on the wheel, the one which Jeremiah spoke of, the vessel that he made of clay was marred in the hands of the potter, so he made it again another vessel, as seemed good to the potter to make it. We're not talking here about "microwave oven type stuff," we are dealing with the Almighty God burning and shaping in his own fire, a fire of his choosing, that up on his completion, the product that finally emerge will be perfect in quality and dimension, that you can now confronts the enemies with boldness and strength, not backing down because of their skills and or toughness, but just because you've been acquainted with the potter who have placed you already on a hot binning wheel. Now you have become unmovable, unshakable, sturdy and strong.

The question is, how very deep is your foundation? How easily can you be uprooted? Will they need to knock you over or must they vigorously dig into the deepest parts of your soil? Paul said, "For other foundation can no man lay than that is laid, which is Jesus Christ. Now if any man built upon this foundation, gold, silver, precious stone, wood, hay, stubble, every man's work shall be made manifest; for the day shall declare it, because it shall be revealed by fire, and the fire shall try every man's work of what sort it is."[5] When your work is tested by fire, will you endure the burning and remain firm even after a hot burning'? A man can talk all he wants and we know that talk is cheap, talk a good one because you've never encountered a great test of faith, what is your experience? Never once have you been tested, you've lived in legacy and enjoyed the best things of life, now it's easy my friends to say all the good stuff since that's all you're accustom to, but, until you've been into the flames to the degree of "testing beyond measure," without been totally consumed, then your talk means nothing. I love sitting down and listening to one that had been through some stuff! Where's the Nelson Mandela? Where's the Martin Luther King, the Sojourner Truth, where is another Mary McLeod Bethume? It is true that the preserving effects of God's fire purifies the saints.

It keeps you going even when conditions are at its worst! Don't just tell me how good you are because things are moving in the best direction, show me how good you can stand when the going gets tough! Show me friends, the proof is in the pudding!

Many will talk but the truth is, all men got a very good talk but you will be tested by fire to see just about what condition you're left in after the fire got out. Yes you will pass through some fire, Isaiah said it best: "when thou walkest through the fire, thou shalt not be burned; neither shall the flame kindle upon thee."[6]

If you will only trust in God, don't ever be afraid of the fire! The three Hebrew boys weren't afraid, they declared, we will not bow! Just do what you have to do Mr. King, the

---

[5] 1 Corinthians 3.11
[6] Isaiah 43.2

God that we serve is greater than fire, he will walk in the fire with us, and we will not be moved by your threats of fire![7] The God that we serve is "a consuming fire!"[8] Tell me of your faith, I'll show you mine! A faith that works, it's no fairytale! It's like fire shut up in my bones!

---

[7] Daniel 3.13-30
[8] Hebrews 12.29

An Anointing that Motivates

Chapter Five

I believe that the anointing power of God, been filled with his spirit is the greatest motivating force for a child of God. The spirit enables power to wit-stand the darts of the wicked. It's that one thing that would move you, or compels you into radical fighting. Regardless of who and how strong the enemy is, it is still the anointing that will destroys the yolk! You will prevail against them because of the anointing.

We have constantly seen all over, those strong willed women like the Prophetess Deborah, that even when the men which were appointed became fearful as they saw in themselves a sense of incapability and inferiority to the might of their enemies and thus were afraid challenging them. We are to appreciate having among us women that are courageous and are moving in the power of the Holy Spirit that when the men are driven by fear and doubts, they'll rise to the occasion showing that it's "Not by might, nor by power, but by my spirit saith the Lord of hosts."[9]

They will not shake nor becoming intimidated by their strength. They are convinced that the God of Heaven will fight their battles. Don't you love to be associated with a woman that is possessed by a level of confidence in the spirit's ability to defeating the enemies and are ever bold in their anointing? Deborah was determine, "I will go into the enemy territory regardless! A courageous woman that will not cop a deal! You can't buy them out, not persuading them into a compromise, they will not bend! A woman that knows how to pray, staying at the feet of the Lord like Jacob, I will not let you go until you bless me! You know a woman that will stay on the wheel until God speaks in his power and are not afraid of the burning, she will say to the men, "Man up!" They are certain that the God of Heaven is incapable of losing a battle.

It is very important that you remember, Barak had already gotten instructions from the Lord, he was given a battle plan which guarantee success, one that would be a sure victory for the Children of Israel, yet, Barak couldn't view from a distant that the God of Israel could never lost a battle, he was in fact, on his side. Some men are as blind and handicap without having the perfect woman of God on his team! To pick a winning team, you will need women that can pray to be at the top of your list! It is prayer that will move God and it is prayer that will stop the battle plans of the enemy. Mary, Sara, Elizabeth, Hannah, Rebekah, Rachel, Ruth and Prophetess Deborah! Man, Barak couldn't see victory even through the eyes of faith, somehow, he would rather accepting defeat. The brother wouldn't dare to walk in

---

[9] Zechariah 4.6

the confidence of his God. Imagine not having Sister Deborah, we thank God that there's such a wonderful sister that possesses that assurance which was rooted in the Spirit's power because Barak said, "look, if you will not go with me, then I will not go!"

Do you need a prestigious sister in your corner? Then find you one like Deborah, bold in her acts of faith, determined in her spirit, filled with the Holy Ghost and fire and will not second guess what the Lord said in his word. Deborah said: "I will surely go with thee: notwithstanding the journey that thou takest shall not be for thine honor; for the Lord shall sell Sisera unto the hand of a woman. And Deborah arose, and went with Barak to Kedesh."[10] Sometimes we must ponder the question, what is really wrong with our brothers today? Looking around, all over, it seem like the sisters thou they are beaten down by cares and headaches, yet they are really out working them. Women are very stirred up in working for God's kingdom than ever before, they are actually fired up, ready and willing to take on extra ordinary challenges. They are the ones that suddenly are functioning with a backbone, holding and keeping the Church of Jesus Christ alive!

Sisters thou frustrated at times, they find it hard to allow the Church of God to go under! At the time when men are to take their position defending the sisters and leading for the cause of Christ, the opposite is happening, women are defending them, fighting for the survival of everything and themselves! Many are even going off in extremely dangerous territory fighting off dangerous giants and wolves where men refuses to tread and are courageous with their efforts. I'm very sadden and sorrowful for the men that will

---

[10] Judges 4.9

fight against our beloved sisters that are wonderful and strong leaders of the Church of God, I guess they don't fully understand the depths of God's power! To be frank with you, sisters are going to the prisons, they are in the field, they are at the hospitals, they are in the subways, you'll find these sisters at the street corners ministering to the lost, they are weeping with those that are weeping, they are helping the oppress, those that are abused, sisters are administering care, they are feeding the hungry, and at any time of the day or night you call these sisters they are available for the cause of Christ! When brothers are sleeping, sisters are on their knees praying, they are on duty twenty four seven, you cannot lose the fight with Deborah on your team! See, all over the world men are falling into a comfort frenzy and the work of God must continue.

They are attached to drugs and a high, tracing the world's pleasure while so much are at stake. My friend, it is the dedicated sisters that are picking up the torch and is courageously running with it to the finish line. Can't you see that the men are carelessly dropping out of the race? Going to the Church house, ninety percent of the saints are the faithful sisters.

Can you imagine if there was no Deborah, what would have been the outcome of the nation of Israel? What a great loss of opportunity to defeating the enemy? When you find a woman that shows strength and resilience by all means just lend her your support because she means business! If you are unable to give the support she needs, then back off don't you dare stand in her way, leave her alone she's a true fighter! In the functioning of God's program, there is neither male nor female, the anointing of God has no boundaries, it's no limitations with God, his plans exceeds all gender barriers!

I know that there are men that will try to counter my assessment of this situation, say it's inaccurate, yet in my heart the truth is burning, I can hardly contain myself. Some men are awfully scared, oh no, it's a man thing, the male ego, their masculinity is been threatened! Buoy, when they would witness a sister having the capabilities to whack havoc on the enemy they are threatened and their manhood gets in the way. Thus they often become or create some stumbling block even fighting against God's spirit. At times God wants to move with power only if some of these powerless men would get out the way so that Deborah can operate in her anointing! Stand up Deborah! Why should you become a stumbling block when you know quite well that you are not equip with the power and boldness required for the task? You are not praying and laboring earnestly for the Spirit's power, you've been busy doing nothing, and you are always engaged but not in Kingdom building. The difference is that Deborah is constantly seeking at the feet of the Lord, she is always hungry and will not be satisfy with just the crumbs, she's always waiting for a full serve, a double portion, and that's why God saw her as trust worthy, very reliable, don't be mad because she's plunging beneath the fount! You can only be alert and ready when you're actually plunging in, there is power beneath the fount! Because that's where you lose all your guilty stains! Deborah said to Barak, "Up! This is the day in which the Lord hath delivered Sisera into thine hand, is not the Lord gone out before thee?"[11]

Doesn't it amaze you that it's the praying sisters that knows the right time to attack? Have you ever met a woman that said, "Don't go to such and such place right now, now is not the right time," but you just wouldn't listen only

---

[11] Judges 14.4

because she's a woman. You refuse to follow her instructions and somehow you live to regret it! A woman will feel in her womb something that just doesn't feel right, she got the kind of natural instinct, only because she's the one that can carry a baby in the womb and God had given her that ability to detect imminent danger, she can just sense it! She felt the pains and the push, she's overly confident when to and when not to. A woman's true instinct, her spirit corresponds with her womb, that's why you can trust the very judgment and decision of a woman of God because she hears from God! So you want to tell me that God made man first, let me tell you something, God places something of a supernatural instinct into a woman that lives in total obedience, something that you will find nowhere else.

Many times, it's true, it's better for you having a woman with you on the battle field, than having ten men. Some men will get you killed by wild beast, sleeping on the job, yet a true woman of God will guard you, she'll defend you, shield you, pray you through, cover you, possess you and each and every step of the way, she'll encourage you, giving you that full support that you need to be successful! So many brothers will give you all the reasons in the world why they think you will fail, they'll find every reason why it's not the right time, they'll delay every opportunities, stalling all your efforts, let's go next week, let's pray about it until you just forget and don't ever want to be bothered, and if they take on the challenge will in more cases provoke you into abandoning your vision, but my God! She, like Deborah, "Up, this is the day!" Yes you need a motivator! One having substance and courage, "What?"

You see, a man will never loose, he'll never fail when the right woman is on his team, and he will be proud because she'll make him proud. You only fail through bad selection!

A woman that is living holy and will not compromise, a set apart vessel, is a treasure for the success of a team. If her only interest is to use her femininity to manipulate and seduce, then that will be a major setback, yet, if her spirits motive is driven to succeed, you will be a man standing strong because you are surrounded by a solid rock!

A story was told of two promising young men. These men were raised by a strong single mother. In fact, their father was deported back to his native and refuses all communications and ties. This mother however, though she had strayed from the fold, rededicated her life to God and experiences the power of God at every point and detail of her sons' lives.

The first son a very brilliant and ambitious boy who seemed to enjoy and had a keen interest in numbers. At first, no one would deny that a journey at the "Wall Street" was inevitable. Mother saw this and was proud knowing that whatever investment in her son would be a guarantee to a profitable pension at her retirement. Things went fairly well, however, after enlisted into a prestigious collage began dating a fine young lady on campus which he met in one study hall. Not only because she was beautiful, but had a lot in common especially their spiritual interest and moral principles. They sprang from the vine. Somehow they had glanced away from God and in their transgressions were introduced to and experimented with drugs of sort. As they continued down this dangerous path, ultimately this created the most damaging setback. That one mistake forces them unfortunately into a life of drug addiction. Finally, they both failed collage, roaming the streets, crushed, wounded and broken, life for them had taken an unfortunate turn, spiraled into oblivion.

It's a very sad picture considering that in one's quest towards success, just one mistake can be so detrimental to the extent that it would snatched away every opportunity of a promised goal. I would without hesitation express my hurts and sorrows just as if they were my own children. Never would I try painting a picture as though the poor daughter should be blamed for this atrocity. It is truly what one can expect turning away from God, reaping the slaughters of the enemy.

As I look at the wonderful turn of events, I was deeply impressed with the way things turned out for the second son. Though he was short of been brilliant and sophisticated as his brother, he had a deep rooted love and appreciation for God. This son truly honored his mother and would be founded constantly in the house of God worshipping, praising and growing intimately with God. Unlike his older brother, he was never possessed with such deal of sophistication, no college make up, he worked at a low key super market, remained humble and lived in restraint. One day after carefully observing him, his local Bishop called him to his office. "Son, I think God is going to reward you for your faithfulness. I watched you and you've been growing immensely and am so very proud of you. I just want you to follow the instructions that am going to give you, God told me that a certain sister in our congregation should become your wife because both of you are young, dedicated to the things of God and is striving seriously for his glory."

That information was very good news for him, so they prayed together, he was very happy, finally the following day he met with his future wife. These young people were later married and over fifteen years they are still living a wonderful life together with three beautiful children, it wonderful home and a small landscaping business.

Not only is this family flourishing well with the blessings of God, they are still actively involved in their local church, doing the work of God and are true witnesses of God's power, saving knowledge and true intervention.

It is true, when we allow God to direct our lives, we will have good success. You must carefully analyze your selection and you must stay under the guiding hands of God so that no good things will be withhold from you. The first brother as you can see, drifted from the true path, shifted from the best plan, "A God's plan" one that would never fail. Educationally, this son might have thought that he had gotten it together, yet, that is a false notion without the Wisdom of God. As he was seeking the success of the world, he began to forsake the God that kept him all those wonderful years. No wonder the Bible said, what does it profit a man to gain the whole world and loses his soul or what would he give in exchange for his soul? Everything that one acquires in this life without the Lord at the center, it is worth nothing! Yet, having obtained nothing on a material spectrum but having richness in God, you can boast about great wealth! If in your search for greatness you will have to leave from the close family tradition, never forget what you've been thought from those wonderful grandmothers and grandfathers, "take Jesus with you everywhere you go!" Having Jesus with you in the far distant of life is a guaranteed success. You will never fall short with Jesus and in the decision making process he will give you the wisdom that you need.

In your pursuit to attaining success, the word of God is the key to unlock doors to prosperity. "This book of the law shall not depart out of thy mouth, but thou shall meditate therein day and night, that thou mayest observe to do according to all that is written therein: for then thou shall make thy way prosperous, and then thou shall have good success. Have not I commanded thee? Be strong and of a good courage; be not afraid, neither be thou dismayed: for the Lord thy God is with thee whithersoever thou goest."[12] Anything else, like the first brother, he had forget that word which was taught to him from his youth and he failed miserable. Especially when we are moving up the ladder, we do need other's that are sound in the word of God that can help us with our decision making. For us to survive the wiles of Satan, we need others! Thank God for the blessed Holy Spirit, that can help us choosing the right people to enrich our lives, those that will be a complete crown unto us. God is still speaking to Bishops and Pastors that are hearing and heeding his voice, those that refuse to lean on their own understanding! It is important that we point our sons to the daughters of Zion. Are there any daughters among thy brethren? Going to colleges are good, yet it's definitely not a ticket to following your own devices! You all have given the responsibilities to continue to walk in the righteousness which you were thought in days of old. Far too many have erred while climbing the ladder of success. Well, you may say, " I can't think locally anymore." It is vital that those you choose to associate with must be Godly! Evil communication corrupts good manners! Many people lives in a gold mine yet, cannot see the gold, went about seeking for gold in diverse places, only that others will spot the gold that he refuses to see from a distant, polish and shine them for God's glory. Don't be mad after you witness the wonders of God's hand. A prophetess like Deborah, is right in your circle, one that you've been rejecting all along, she loves the

---

[12] Joshua 1.8-9

Lord, sold out completely for his service and is ready for you! She will tell you, "Up! For this is the day, it's an anointing which motivates.

Behold a True Fighter

Chapter Six

In one of the Apostle Paul's eloquent writing, he uses an essentially important analogy. "But we have this treasure in earthen vessels that the Excellency of the power may be of God and not of us." This powerful sentiment spells out the most fascinating revelation that the disenfranchised, the dysfunctional and often times those that are looked on as insignificant are the ones that hold within them this God given "treasure in earthen vessels."

Do you not know that Satan is busy working around the clock creating strongholds to keep those treasures dormant, that your value and potential would be reduce to its lowest degree? It is undisputed that having the understanding of God's power, we can come to the place of recognizing that the most precious diamonds are found in the strangest places of the world.

Somewhere in the rough terrains of Africa, in cities, streets and towns, likewise in many parts of the world which often times are less likely to having any viable contribution to our world. An outcast people that are somewhere in the slums and ghettos in rural communities, where various diamonds are left hopeless, like dry bones waiting helplessly for a resurrection. Certainly, God will one day move into these places to make the perfect cuttings. Never look on bones that seems lifeless and simply bypass them, thinking they are without worth. God is at work and just a breath of his nostrils those bones will live to declare God's abundant glory.

Paul said, God uses the base things of this world to confound the wise and he also uses the foolishness of this world to confound the simple. One that's been to the bottom, been rejected, a refused product, we know that they are essential with God. I've seen men whom have been rejected by his wife, many wives that are found to be despised by the one's they love. They suffers mentally and emotionally, lived a life of constant strains and scars. Yet I have seen how God's power was able to pick up by the thousands many of these wonderful saints, placing in them his spirit and how we marvel at the wonders of his immutable power, because from a distraught, melt down and ruing life had been restored and those that were on the brink of death, hath given up on life are risen up with wings and are proclaiming, " I shall not die but live to declare the goodness of God!" Yes, out from the dust many are still rising up!

Recently I was engaged in a regular conversation with a friend of mine. He loves the taste of coffee, which he must have sometimes between eight to fifteen times per day. Have you ever saw a real coffee plant? "No!" he replied. I told him, if you should ever see a real coffee plant and notice the process through which coffee is cultivated to the point of finally making it into your home and on your table, with its fine taste and aroma, you would never again be so abusive to the coffee that you claim that you love. When something is of such great peculiarity, you should contribute to its enhancement and not to its destruction. People deserve a chance regardless of the degradation that somehow they've encountered, there still remains, "a treasure in earthen vessel."[13] One may never comprehend fully, some of what life has given many, reducing them to ashes. Yet beneath the heap of ashes, should we had not been so cold and longed for compassion, we'd gladly seek after them, finding out that any are beneath these ashes screaming out for hope and a sense of purpose. Have you ever thought for a moment that behind our perfumes and deodorant, we all possess the capacity to decay, should we not use these freshness for a day, we realizes how stink we can all get.

    The reason we are so cold and abusive to each other, especially to those dearest to us, is the fact that we are not fully appraised of where God, the creator has taken us from, and how he transformed us into such a beautiful image. Think about it, we are sitting in heavenly places by Christ Jesus! But yes, if we should know who we truly are, we would begin to look at the beauty that resides in others and appreciate our great God for such a wonder given to mankind. Yes, we will never understand fully and to the greatest extent, the process through which great men are made to be great. For some reasons it just doesn't appear as though they were actually placed in the fire, you look on great men and you immediately assume that he just got great because of good fortune or maybe by chance. You must recognize that he's been through the fire, and in that fire God kept him preserved, he's been refined and as you look at him, not a trace of defects can be found. You look at men that's

---

[13] 2 Corinthians 4.7

been in the desert, they've been through afflictions, yes, men that have trodden through deep waters, been beaten and abused, stripped of their dignity, imprisoned, wounded, been oppressed, going through "hell and hot water" and many times are dealt with unjustly.

These men suffer the greatest magnitude of sufferings, a tenth degree suffering for real! Yet through it all, these men are still here, except for all those that have gone on to glory, to be with Jesus, whose memories and spirits, most importantly, their great legacies which remain in our lives forever that motivates and strengthens us! Those that are still here none-the-less and are still maintaining their integrity, they are still lifting their heads above the water, though others may have wanted them to hang their heads down, they are still here! Glory be to God! And they are still vigilant in fighting.

It is true that no great men had gotten great without paying a huge price. It is costly to rise to greatness, tearing down barriers, beating all odds, pushing and pulling through mediocrity, having the determination not to be distracted by traps set in place by the enemy to tear you to pieces. Many times, you'll have to be burned and suffer excruciating pains as the process of your elevation seem realistic. Can you imagine King David raises to greatness without going through his stuff? We're talking about near death experiences, looking at death in the face many times, yet determined to live with resolve and conviction. How about Joseph? Just imagine these young men coming up in life, and not having their unfortunate experiences, they would have lost their focus and their ability to see visions. Men were made to fight and conquer the impossibilities and making them possible. Trials were good for Moses, they were good for Abraham, the Apostle Paul had gotten his anointing through the many pains and test he encountered, yet every victory and triumph were strong motivation to press towards the goal. Martin Luther fought, Nelson Mandela fought! You might not be where you want to be, but one thing you do, like Yawl said, you put the pass behind and press towards the mark of the prize of the high calling of God! What did all the many patriarchs of the faith, our founding fathers did? My God! They pressed! Not allowing any major setback to distract them of their God given progress, they refuse from harboring the tendency to fail and they pressed!

The price that they paid were huge, astronomically huge, very costly, and even to the point of death! They are the true heroes of the faith, through unyielding strength they subdued Kingdoms, wrought righteousness, obtained promises, stopped the mouths of lions, they quenched the violence of fire, yes, these are heroes that escaped the edge of the sword, out of weakness they were made strong. They my friends, waxed valiant in fight, they are the ones that turned to flight the armies of the aliens. We are even mindful that even women that were strong forces to be reckoned with in the battle for our eternal victories. We are told that they received their dead, raised back to life while others were tortured not accepting deliverance that they might obtain a better resurrection and others had trials of cruel mocking and scourging, of bonds and imprisonment. Some were even stoned, some were even sawed asunder, they were tempted, they were slain with the sword, they wondered about in sheep skins and goat skins. It is true that some were destitute, afflicted, tormented wondering in the deserts, in mountains, in caves and dens of the earth. Yet we crumble into hopelessness at the thought of carrying a cross. Are you crazy, slap me in the face, the way they slapped Jesus and it is war! Yet the Great King of Glory not only was slapped, they spat in his face, mocking him, gave him vinegar to drink, not only that, he carried a bloody cross, one that was heavy and burdensome and he had not retaliated! Think about the many fruits to be yielded from enduring sufferings. Once we endure, cultivating from their examples a back bone to fight, not giving up under pressure but standing in the fire believing that the Almighty God is yet standing in the blazing flames with you, then tomorrow you can look back and say, it was well worth it, because Jesus has done it, so could you, glory to God!

God has a way of making things the way they are, many times at least, it is quite conflicting and complicated in regards to the course which the Lord chooses for us. When not focusing on its complexities too much but rather, putting our trust in God, we will pull through them, moving on in victory and facing with confidence our assignment to put us to that next level, as we possess a winning attitude. Why did Jesus have to die so that you and I can live? These are the great mysteries, some things are without explaining. You endured, you overcame, now it's time for climbing the ladder moving on to the next level. Will you be able to master the many challenges that are involve at the height of the next level of your assignment, if all you can do now is to whine and complain at this round? I guess you still need to stay in the fire some more, there's still some burning left to do and a regular fight is twelve rounds, you must hang in there and fight. One reality is, everyone's not made to go through the same burning, some will be on top of the stove while other's must be locked inside the oven. Some just need to be burned, while others must be baked! "Johnny Cake!" It's no mistake for God, you get mad as you are going through your stuff, yet God is on the right course with your life. You will rejoice at the end as you see the wonders of God's miracle working power manifested in your life.

Suffering is an effective door to greatness, Jesus suffers and after he endures he was exalted. We as a people in today's society, do not like to struggle to reach our goal, we do not like to journey in a battle and win in a twelve round fight. We want to go in the ring and knock down our opponent with one jab, then cheer with our fans as we go off to celebrating. That is easy, yet, the great battle for life is never won so easily when our opponents are like giants, they are spiritual wickedness, principalities and powers. For us to win, it takes jabbing, it takes wrestling, it takes endurance to the point of us taking some serious beat down, but the attitude we should employ is never to surrender because to retreat means failure.

Strong and courageous men that have been through hell but never quit, they survived by the power of God that the world can see, know and fear the true and living God. Beloved, if you can't bear the cross, just don't expect to wear the crown! Why did Jesus suffer the way he did? Christ didn't have to carry a bloody cross, he didn't have to take a slap by wicked sinners. The Lord of glory didn't have to walk the streets of Golgotha, (Gethsemane). Christ could have forgone all the brutal attacks, calling thousands of angels but he humbled himself, took the cruel and torturous whippings, nailed to a cross and died a cruel death.

If you want a crown, gladly carry your cross, none of us can expect to just walk into greatness and not suffer a great deal, when even Christ himself "must needs go through Samaria!" God's only son suffered the way he had before he was exalted. That's why after he endured, the bible said, "God has highly exalted him and has given him a name that is above every name, that at the name of Jesus, every knee shall bow and every tongue shall confess that Jesus Christ is

Lord!" The prestige comes after the scorns, after the rejections, and yes, after the whippings.

There was never and will never be a prophet that endured the pains like Jesus. Moses went through some stuff, David, Joseph, the Apostle Paul and many others throughout history. Yet they can't touch Jesus. The fact is they all died and are buried. The bones of many prophets of old still remain underneath the ground. But the Lord Jesus though he suffered and died, we can testify that he's risen from the dead! Christ is no longer in the grave. After it was all over, Jesus said: "I am he that liveth, and was dead; and behold, I am alive for evermore."[14] In fact, Jesus our Lord is in glory sitting at the right hand of God interceding for us. He is still on our side, helping us, the common people like you and me.

Though you might be suffering, if you continue in the fight, if you will just remain steadfast, you know that after a while, you will arise! The grave of your situation will not keep you under, because of the risen Christ, he will burst the tomb that you found yourself in and in three days you will arise and live! Fight, be a true fighter, then you'll enjoy the pleasure of a powerful resurrection. Your light afflictions are certainly necessary, which is but for a moment. For they work for you a far more exceeding and eternal weight of glory. While you look not at the things which are seen. But at the things which are not seen: for the things which are seen are temporal; but the things which are not seen are eternal.

One day you too can stand to proclaiming your emancipation proclamation like Jesus our Lord, "I've made it! I've overcome! I have triumph!

---

[14] Revelation 1.18

Battered in the Ring

Chapter Seven

It must be a lie thinking you're unable to fight like the Prophets of old and become victorious in your effort. Contrary to that thought, I solidly believe that we are possessed by God with that same divine power dwelling in us to conquer giants. The awesome God that we are serving never change, He in fact, is the same yesterday, today and forever! Let's face the facts, the prophets of old had fought many ridged battles and won. Oh what great battle plans were wrought through many prayers. They prevailed against the giants. They prevailed against the wolves. They even put great snakes into running. Prayer! Let's think about it for a while, the Fathers of the faith subdued Kingdoms, they battled great sharks and whales. As I look at the word of God I observed keenly my faithful brother David. This wonderful brother that I love, he in fact was, "a man after God's own heart," he expressed his strong love for God in so many ways, in fact, esteeming Him more than his necessary food. Yet, with that kind of love for his God, one must admit, he was just a man like any other man, like us, he was subject to like passion, yet the weapon of prayer allowed him to keep on persevering and glory be to God, he had never lost a battle!

David had a major problem, something of great proportion to the extent that if there's any truth, most of us are possessed in some way or the other, having "a woman problem." In our journey of faith, we will have to fight through some of our most pressing problems and remain faithful to God. With David, no one could possibly think that he, a friend of God, the apple of his eye, devoted, the beloved man David, knowingly or intelligently took a glance away from God, an act that would be detrimental and would ruin his salvation. David fell into an adulterous and murderous life which caused him a great deal in his service to God.

One can never underestimate the power of the enemy attacking the anointed of God. Hear was a great leader, filled with power and zeal even from birth, clothes with potential flowing from his innermost being. A shepherd boy whose ability was known by God, we may asked, "Why on earth could one as close to God as David finds himself trapped into such ambiguous behavior?" It's fair to suggest that the road which David travels, not many are so blessed to tread, he was in fact a hero in his ability to confront the enemy.

We can never think it strange that one can be so close to God that he is completely safeguarded from the traps of Satan, a temptation so grave can come upon a child of God and when you least expect you fall squarely on your face, but for the grace of God! In the word of God, we are told that David fought and won many great battles. Yes, he did conquer many great nations of the world, and what does it take for such a great man to fall into sin? Simple, seeing a woman taking a shower. You can never tell what strategy the enemy will use, he never used a great military army to tear down a man of God. He will use the strangest thing we would least expect. Certainly we can attest to the fact that David was no stranger to women, he had gotten plenty of them, but how was he feeling at the time he was alone?

We can never be ignorant of the schemes of the devil for he's after everyone that calls upon the name of the Lord! Strong men are slain by her, don't you dare think that he can't get you, you are never too slick, you just missed her by a leap and unfortunately, our brother David was at the wrong place at the wrong time, and got caught in the web! We must remember that we are only so strong until we are actually tested.

What will we do when the great test comes our way without notice? We never know if we will act just like the man David did. Even a king can be tested beyond measure. Where does your weakness lie? So after analyzing the capabilities of this great King David my beloved brother, I saw the human frailties in all of us, that same element which will capture our attention at the moment we least expect. As we recollect in our own existence, so many wonderful men of God just make some bad decisions. Not all the time going on the roof, not all the time seeing her taking a shower but whatever banana peel the enemy places in our path can be the great test and we must fight to protect our soul's salvation. I believe that we can win some of these fights, we are able to win them all when we stay under the umbrella of the divine covering of the Lord. It is still amazing that in every fight we are faced with, the Almighty God sees us through them. In a world filled with tests and temptations a champion for God will at some time suffer "shipwreck" of some sought.

King David was not actually out looking for a temptation to befall him. The poor brother was not looking for trouble. He did not wake up in the morning saying, "Well, tonight I will seek to commit the sin of adultery." Is there a symptom for adultery? As we live our lives daily, we see things that spontaneously creep up on us depending on our personal experiences. I can in my own spiritual imagination visualize David's intentions for that day, no doubt he was very excited about his men winning the war. As he received wonderful reports of their accomplishments, he might just take a stroll on the roof top to get relief and fresh air, to get away from all the hassles of the day. No evils intended, yet, even after having good intentions, we can be tested beyond measure, just stopping by to say hello can lead to a life of sin which the impacts can be devastating.

David's men were at the very climax of the war and as the Commander in Chief, sexual gratifications would have been the last thing on his mind until he was presented with the test. Admittedly, we men do have sexual thoughts on a regular basis during the course of the day. We are cautioned to walk in the spirit. We must be careful not to allow our spirit to be interrupted by beautiful objects that will cause us to sin.

A fight in the spirit can sometimes be lost, due to images that the flesh, creates to diminish our mind and conscience that suddenly we are caught in the clutches of lusts, taken our minds to places we'd almost thought to be impossible. Great people having great plans for their lives are tripped up all the time. The word of God speaks clearly along this line, "A just man falleth seven times, and riseth up again: but the wicked shall fall into mischief."[15] At first

---

[15] Proverbs 24.16

glance, I would have thought that some falls are only for certain people, not for the great saints that are close friends of God. In my sometimes narrowness, I would have thought that these things can only happen to the "bad" or in most cases, "the shaky ones", those sometimes "church goers." Most holy saints will not even look on a sister taking a shower. Oh, they'd look away as fast as though this would mean the worst sin to be committed. Yet, the mere looking is not a sin. Once you look and cannot look away, something that won't allow you to move, it's a trap! Watch out, banana peel!

In our society, we sometimes places our leaders at such a plateau and once they fall, we are overtaken with grief and despair. Men are all prone to fall and we are all standing only by the grace of God, not any good deeds that you've done. Not even our great attitude and strength, or our ability to ignore the roof. Something on the other side of the fence can sneak upon us and we get caught by surprise.

What is our attitude like when the lights go out? Are we the same or do we sometimes harbor in us a slight reflection of the "David-like syndrome?" Maybe if nights were to ever turn into day, many would be shocked that the best people we see in the day are sometimes not the same in the night! It doesn't matter at all that they may act as they're great giants in the faith. Unintentionally, the good are stock with a certain degree of weaknesses that only God is able to eradicate from their "Adamic nature.

How dare a great musician so anointed and filled with the Holy Ghost make an error such as this? Have we ever seen in our choir a man or woman so anointed, yet is always caught in the web of sin? The enemy is after you, try to live a Godly life and he will not resist one bit until he is successful at his crafts. Is it too hard believing that at a man's strongest point he may be just as susceptible to his weakest. A fight can knock over a giant but as a true fighter you can get up and be strong again. True fighters get up from where they fall and fight again for God's glory. In the Church we see from time to time those that make you think that, if you ever see a sister taking a shower you'll just pass by without a simple gaze.

Walking on the roof top and seeing a glisten can draw the attention and alert anyone that something is going on over there. Water running and wet hair is beautiful and one of the most appealing sights for a brother is a sister taking a shower anyway. That will mess with the mind for days! The most noble, self-righteous man that exist will look, turn away, then look, scratch his head, look to the sky, Lord! Have mercy upon me, then look again. The first look was not as bad, the second one is where the lust comes in and you get stuck at the second look. A state of confusion crept in and you're at a place of no return. Someone often said, "it is better that you don't look at all." But the first thing is to master that "not looking attitude." I can just imagine what my poor, rich brother David went through, a struggle, a war that he himself not even realized was there.

I still believe that David sincerely would never want to be involve in that kind of mess, yet, at the Weakest moment of one's life, just when we are in the most vulnerable state, a beauty shows up at that place, the enemy is just laughing, "I know he's going to do it, I know it." That cunning old Devil, I hate him, don't you hate that old dragon? He loves to just destroy the people of God and cause us to make a fool of our wonderful self. What! I believe to some extent that some temptations can be tolerated and some can be excused, some you're just caught off guard, I guess, what you think? When you look from a man's point of view, those hormones are quite active, they sometimes run seriously wild, acting crazy and at the moment of distress. Only the good Lord can come to your rescue, the itch, the scratch and you better believe it, "the blood swiftly running warm in your veins!" How excellent and unique we are made by a wonderful God, our bodies are so very special, we have such great feelings, emotions and the joy of sexuality, we just don't quite understand the art of managing such gifts.

Sexuality is such a sacred gift from God. But it can get us into trouble, oh my God! Have you ever been down and out? Have you ever been going through a cloud, have you ever experienced moments of emptiness and just the pains of life's burdens? A very good sexual experience will in most cases quench the fire and that's why Paul tells us, "it's better to married than to burn." Marriage is honorable! Married brother, you better do it and stop that burning! Enjoy a splendid feeling that is safe and secure and paid for, legal! You are legit when married, you get that soothing relief, relaxation, leaving you with shavers and my God! A special kind of " tongues" not heard in the worship services, screams and hollers, that's all right she is yours friend, bought and paid for, not David's. Thus, you develop a language that only you can speak when the heat of passion gets hot.

How could you even begin to judge King David? Being a man wise in his affairs, administers justice well. I know it might sound unreasonable but, most of the greatest men even in today's society, are often heard of committing blunders. This is an indication that we all need Jesus Christ to shield us from the many traps of Satan. Let us not fake it, but, the Holy Spirit does not strive with men at all times for real, the things that I don't want to do that I do and the things that am to do that I do not. Woe is me, how wretched I am?

Sometimes it's very strange that at the moment you get off your knees, even in the peak of your prayers, the enemy comes in when you least expect it taken your mind to some of the strangest places that you've never dreamed of going! Do I have a witness'? You are there praying your best prayer, having a good time with God, rejoicing and filled with victory. Then suddenly, An "uppercut" knocks you over, yes, this is the way Mr. Satan work's, just lays in the cut waiting for you, "oh", he said, "see you having a good time on your knees, I got something better for you, I know you had a good time with the Father?" He is subtle, he knows the right time to attack and the right strategy.

He brought back all the pass, and makes sure that they stays in your mind. "You remember that girl on the roof? She was fine taking that shower, wasn't she? Then he even produce a picture of her in your mind, bringing confusion and a host of war in the spirit man. How very awful it is that even when you try, and try to live the holy life that you know God honors, he will find a way to penetrate your mind and spirit. That's why we must be a fighter at our best, for at that time only a great fighter can overpower the strong man, we must be able to wrestle and throw him flat on his face. Without that, you'll find that soon you forget that wonderful moment that you had with the Lord and in your mind, he'll take you on a hunting trip, looking, seeking and in his web, you'll never be able to detect, until you finally realized where you are and what is going on.

I thought somebody once said, "When trouble comes at you, a child clothes will fit you." David felt as though he was a child in the state he found himself. You know that you are filled with the Holy Ghost and all, sanctified and all, but, at the weakest moment, only by God's grace that you can actually stand. The energy that one must exert to sustain the faith walk, we can never underestimate, we can never no matter how hard we try to, we can never shop for an energy boost to keep on tract with your Christian journey. It is completely impossible living the life in your human strength, but we can live a victorious life by living in the power and strength of the Lord. It is what we must do, throw ourselves on his mercies and rely on him to take us through.

I have observed my brothers many times, and I've watched their sincerity. They love the Lord so very much, but that one hurdle, that one situation is a deterrent, they just can't get over that hump. We would never want to violate the holy temple of our body. Not willfully giving in to the lust and temptations of our lives. It's a great fight, and it's one that we must win! The attitude is to "flee!" and by all means we must avoid the roof top completely. On the roof top there are things there that you really do not want to see, things that aren't good for your spirit and a holy man will send for her as the aroma of freshness hits you, just coming out of the shower, oil and cinnamon, spice and all kinds of fragrance, one sniff you'll never be able to resist.

The roof top is good, you can spy your surroundings and yes, the fresh air and view of God's creation makes it the most splendid place to be. Yet, on the roof looking down, whatever distractions, we just can't give place to the devil. We must keep a clear motive when we find ourselves on top of a roof, what are we there looking for? Sin will caught you off guard if we are not focused on our real goals. How can I do such a great wickedness and sin against my God? David cries, "have mercy on me oh God!" "Create in me a clean heart oh God!" "Search me oh God!" These are the deepest cries of a poor sinner humble bowing before a merciful God. Certainly he will hear a contrite and a broken spirit, he said, "he will not despise."

We are at times never prepared as people of God for a sudden attack in the sexual arena as these attacks are never always planned but creeps on the saints. As we can observe in the Scriptures, the sister was to the great extent caught off guard, presumed innocent indeed. As reasonable people, we shouldn't believe that she was to be blamed. Had you been in that predicament what or how would you react as you stands before the King? A very difficult and unusual situation I would guess. If she should refuse, it could be detrimental as she was a woman dealing with a King in those days. Consequences could amount to capital punishment, stoning to be exact! Would you really want to be stoned as a woman? Well, most would say, I'll just do this and face the consequences of my sin and make up with my husband, as it turns out there was much more of a big problem, a problem of great proportion. At least, Bathsheba was only taking a shower, can a woman just take a shower, for crying out loud'? She was minding her own business, taking care of herself for her husband's return, and rightly so, the best thing a sister could do for her man away in the battle field. Beautifying herself for her soldier! Can you imagine what was going through her mind as she feels the water running down her body? "My husband will be home soon!"

This sister was actually saying, "when Uriah, my husband comes home, he will definitely love the way that I look, feel and smell." She was getting the tan, the spices and all the nice stuff that girls uses, those perfumes, those hair pieces, can you imagine, like a bride preparing for her bridegroom, the joy and pleasure waiting for her soldier makes the shower even more fun. Actually, how nice it was just taking a long and lonely shower, how it could ease the mind and divert certain urges and take the mind to a place of relaxation. The last thing on her mind was to willfully abort her pleasure of spending a celebrated moment with her husband arriving from a jungle, fighting in David's war. She prayed for his safety, she prayed for his protection, gazing into the heavens, "I wish that this war was over today! " She was just reasoning with herself and enjoying her dreams at the same time. As I pictured Bathsheba, humble, honest and like a virgin, only now the lust infested David would seriously manipulated her into such an act of deception.

The heart of man is deceitful above all things and desperately wicked, who can know it, said Jeremiah.[16] How long does it take for the heart to turn and imagine wickedness? Lust when it's conceive bring forth sin, sin when it is finish bring forth death, said James. It all starts in the mind and so quickly, suddenly a guilty soul not expecting nothing of the ordinary, just acted like a fool. No Christian is completely immune from a fetal attack of Satan, it's one of the things that we all inherited from our Father Adam, it's in our nature, although sometimes it won't surface, it remains dormant until triggered by the right temptation that puts the shaking on what we have thought was dead. Remember that, though a thing might seem dead, if the root is not taken out completely, it has the capacity to grow again. A volcano, without an eruption for years may erupt when least expected. David hasn't been on the roof in a long time, so why would he worry? He may have thought to himself: "there's never been a temptation there before, so I guess it's safe there." Never having an occasion on the roof top, so your limitations have never been tested. Can you actually believe that you really possess such a David like mentality? You are really a man that is so close to God and doing everything to please God as you sing and dance like David. Worship like the brother and conquered many giants just like your big brother,

---

[16] Jeremiah 17.9

yet, underneath all that, you are as weak as your brother, having a problem like your brother. How can one know for sure his capabilities, since he never encountered a severe test? You fall but you get up, you're punched, kicked and bruised, yet it all had no bearings on the man of God.

I know what it's like calling out to God for mercy, just like brother David. Knock down cold, yet a cry for mercy from the deepest part of the soul, reaches to the heavens and God hears and responds. "Against you, you only have I sinned!" Tell me, isn't God merciful? O yes he is! David was not left alone for dead, he was still a man of God's own heart, just a weary soul attacked by a deadly enemy. Do you see yourself having a David like infection that only can be cured by the power of God? Are you still holding on to God even with your struggle? The fight is not over when you are knocked down, you must fight even harder to get up out of that condition. God is still giving strength to those who calls upon him.

Over these years I have seen so many that had patted themselves in the back then point out the faults and weaknesses of others, they mocked and in laughter, putting down many, making themselves to appear superior, yet they themselves not knowing that they also are possess with a demon in their life that needs to be rebuked. Don't ever go on praising yourself too much, your day will come to be tested. Men are weak and we are a people that are now weaker than David, at home having the most beautiful wife, getting everything done to make you happy.

Bathsheba may not have been the most beautiful woman that David has ever crossed, she doesn't have to be fine, and all that matters sometimes is that she is a woman, we just fold! Beauty, they said, is in the eyes of the beholder and many times we'd be shocked at some of the Women that causes us to tripped up, (shame on you buddy!) It was just one of those moments, you know, bad! Satan will present someone to us at a time when we get weak and she looks so good, until the actual thing happens you finally realize that you were tricked. As long as we are not willing to ask the one that is bigger than us to fight for us we will never be a winner, all the fights we had in our lives, and lost them because we thought that we could do it by ourselves.

Let God fight with us and for us and we will win! The war will never seize, it's an ongoing battle, the flesh after the spirit, the spirit after the flesh, and although we are often in the spirit it seems like the stinking flesh is always winning. Paul said, "The thing that I want to do that I do not, and, that which I don't want to do that I do, oh wretched man I am!"[17] For real, you'd never have the slightest inclination of doing evil, yet evil silently pops up and at the most vulnerable state that one finding himself will determine the outcome, you might have to put up a fight to stand, don't just give in and die, a fighter will live!

Tragically, some sisters might think, "well, my husband is at war, I'm going to wait until he gets home." You may even be totally committed to the man in your life and would never do anything to hurt him, even in his absence, "I would never do that to my man, I will just wait." That's what most sisters say. That's good intention, oh yea, you must remember the enemy is not fair when they fight, they are subtle, after you've won every test that comes your way, Satan knew it, he knows that you are standing strong, walking in integrity, trying hard not to defile your garments. Yes and these urge keeps coming, but you always find the

---

[17] Romans 7. 15, 24

strength and the courage to shun them off. And so here comes Mr. Satan studying his plan well, okay Sister, I've sent two local men at you, you fought off well, I've sent you two other soldiers, since you are accustom to soldiers, you still didn't fall for it, I've sent you two Captains, trying to see if you'd rather the higher ranks, you're still playing hard ball, "girl, you're getting me mad!" Aright, I got something for you, let me see you get out of this one.

See, a plan that is carefully executed by the enemy will force you into doing things that otherwise you wouldn't have done, Satan instead sent at you, the King himself! Will you be brave enough to reject the King? There is serious consequences in rejecting the King, you don't want to deal with that, now what will you do? When the King see you baby, he in love with what he saw, and what he'll do is send his men for her! Now what will you do, tell the King, not now? Most likely, you will comply with the King's request, "I need some of that thing, what's up?" So here's Bathsheba, I can imagine she resented the idea somewhat, and I do believe that she might even have thought that it was a joke. She said to herself, "Maybe King David was only testing my commitment to my husband just to see what my reaction would be."

Standing in the King's presence, what a great struggle that was. This was not America in today's world, which would have created a scandal of the century, they would fry Obama had such an act occurred while he's the President. So she reluctantly approached the King, she wonders, weighing her options, and with fear and trembling, gave in to the Kings demands.

Well, how many times as humans, that we find ourselves trapped, in various addictions, being overtaken by drugs, liquor, prostitution, gangs or any other such things which the enemy throws at us to the point that he robs us of the joy that we should have. Can you just imagine on the job, you know that you don't want to be fired, you know that times are tough, the bills to be paid, children have to eat and wear clothes. It's easy to say, "Not now!" Yet as you're confronted with the situation, you never can tell, a pay increase is always good, are you crazy? Health benefits, promotions, just to name a few. Don't think that people don't compromise themselves for benefits when they are available, it's human nature to feed into the desires of the flesh. You just might be surprised at what some folks do, especially when the stakes are good? They'll rip you apart and tear you until you realize you are wiped out completely of money and valuables. That dragon, Satan, he is conniving, whenever you are bombarded by him, for some it's a "rap." They can never get back up! Compromising as a child of God is a no, because the fruits of compromising can be deadly, many lives are lost due to this mistake, and lost without hope.

Jesus said: "For what shall it profit a man, if he shall gain the whole world, and lose his own soul?"[18] What will you give in exchange for your soul? A promotion, a few thousand dollars, a house or a car? Are all these material things really worth it my friend? Not one iota! Don't even make excuses either, it simply not worth it. Make sure that you are alert and always looking out for those nice propositions, Satan wraps them into expensive papers and presenting them into ways that are hard to ignore, yet still, mother said it best, "all that glitters is not gold!" Hello! Look at what is coming behind these beauty. God is still your provider, he will make a way for you that is the God we

---

[18] Mark 8.36

serve. Don't just seek for an easy way out. The easy way out is to go to God in prayer, he hears the cries of the sinners too, don't believe the hype, he will not despise the afflicted when you come to him in sincerity. I often sympathizes with David, just like any other person. We should all be compassionate, David after all accepts his faults, though he was sadly reluctant to a certain degree, yet he finally came to the place of accepting the responsibilities later. I admire David's attitude and that's the reason why God loves him the way he did. This man was repentant. His attitude towards repenting was for real and without hesitation. He would go to God, and say "have mercy upon me!"

In my time, I've learned that the greater the responsibilities, are, the greater the attacks, and since the enemies won't send an army at a local drug dealer, he'll carefully choose the best suited weapon based on the kind of mission he's aiming at. As you can see from the word of God, David was out of place, neglecting his station, he certainly should have been with his men at war, yet, when you are been set up by the enemy, you will even reject your own obligations by staying on the roof.

Beloved, it's that easy to turn over your responsibilities to someone else without personally analyzing such a decision. Even the best leaders can be forced into such errors. Many times, it might even seem like the best thing to do not knowing that Satan is the one behind that plan to actually destroy your credibility. As you sit idle, wasting your time, watch out there's a trap coming! Satan is about to surprise you by giving you something that you will regret. They said, "Idle time" is "Satan's time." and here he comes, "go on the roof, there's nothing else going on right now!" Just so simple, without warning, not even the slightest inclination that trouble was brewing. Brother's, a walk on the roof is nothing good for a man on a mission, just don't be led as a lamb to the slaughter! One simple act turns out to be a big old flame in the burning bush, and this sin spreads! You encounter something simple not understanding the root, somehow we forget that we are to shun the very appearance of evil, we thought, "Oh! It's alright, I can handle that."

How many times do we say that? "I can handle that, it's easy." Only we never read the fine prints and the warning label which indicates danger, so We've learnt the hard way that sin starts out with a tiny pebble then gradually it expands and stretches like rubber, it stretch and stretch until that thing swells out of control. My God, a sore left untreated is likely to break out into a deep wound and you will most likely feel its impact. Sin is dangerously contagious avoid it at every cost my friends.

Don't Neglect Your Station

Chapter Eight

Fighting the giant sometimes means, never neglecting your station, you must never stay idle. There is always something we can do to occupy our time to keep the enemy away. If you stay active and do something positive, the attacks of the enemy will be minimized. One thing that must be done is to support our counterparts and never leaving them to do it alone. One hand washes the other and they both washes your face. In fact, no man is an island, according to the famous saying.

We need our brothers, had David been in the company of his brothers at the time, he would have been safe. Certainly, his brothers would say, "David, not so, that's just not going to work! Remember that's the wife of Uriah." Once you are alone, either you are accompanied by the Holy Spirit or you invite the enemy to infiltrate your mind. What will you do when you're alone? Will you be alert, swift enough to detect his devices? While we look at sin, it gets more enticing, and like David we might use our status wooing people into sin, and the effects can be devastating. If you are not connected you will never see it coming. As Mothers have said it best, "trouble doesn't set like rain." If we can tell when trouble is about to strike, we would be a fool getting caught into its web. We should do everything possible to avoid them. There is no alarm, no trumpets or warning signs announcing trouble, yet we can hear the voice of God when he speaks, and the fact is that Satan cannot speak as clear as the master, our heavenly Father.

Somehow in our society it is plain that an attack is consistently after our sons, not just from the time of Pharaoh, not just from the time of King Herod. Moses should have been wiped out and that's the plain truth. Jesus should have been dead way before his crucifixion. In every walk of life, the enemy has made a decree that once a king is about to rise up, he must do everything in his power to destroy his destiny, and he will not stop short until he is successful at that task. The Kings in our lives need direction and without that they will fall into the brutal traps of Satan. Have we began to see and admire the wonderful gifts and talents that our sons and daughter's possess? They are given gifts from God to enrich their lives, but Satan wants to over throw them before they are even manifest. Our children are blessed with that same gifts and abilities that David was graciously anointed with. Some are hidden inside, waiting for the right time and person to help them make it happen. They are great musicians, great leaders, Kings and Queens that are right there in your homes waiting to be seated on their throne, waiting to be crowned.

The enemy will take the fathers away from them prematurely as a means of destroying them. As the enemy watches your children, he already detects their full potential. Have you heard your children singing that song in the shower? Have you seen them handling that ball? Have you heard them speak, the words they uses and their articulate styles and attitude? God's anointing is real strong on their lives and the enemy knows that. But what do you think? Kill every firstborn! That's what the enemy wanted. Let the Kings die young! A lie from the devil.

Great Kings suffer the greatest trials. Why do you see your sons going through those test? It's not that he was a bad boy, it's just that he is anointed and the enemy will not quit raising up the forces of hell and all kinds of demonic forces up against him.

If he was after David in such a way, beloved, he's after your sons! He will not rest my friend, until every single one of them falls by the wayside. A king can prosper all his life but the devices are laid up against him, and if he ever gets off the right path, there it is. His days are numbered, it's final! Do you believe that your son was really a crack head by his own will? No! He didn't take up the guns for the hell of it, it was an attack to take out the King in him. You bet believe it. Satan blinds him from his true potential. Turning him into an "effeminate." Can't identify himself, wants to be a king but is forced to act like a Queen, just plain confused, not the thing that he really wants to do. If we should assess most of our men that have suffered severe downfalls, just check out his pass anointing. He was so good at everything he touched, he was wreaking havoc on the enemy's territory! That's why the devil makes a pledge to completely take him out before his time.

The devil puts shades on every calamity and he presents them to our children , yes our wonderful boys and precious baby girls that was raised with a bright future, he presented them in the best form there is, so that once you are glued in the dark you are doomed for life. Wonder where are your children today? Is your son waiting to be crowned or is he making the wrong decision letting down his guard. You got the opportunity to stop him in his tracks, go get him now! By the power of God, go find your sons right now! When a King is fallen under corruptible stronghold, it is never the local sisters that is used to his destruction. The high society ladies are many times used by the devil as a lethal weapon against the anointing of God. Satan is drawn to power, a sweet irresistible piece of money, how eager the enemy is to get you off course, he'll provide a mansion on a hill, decking it with all the accessories the human mind can conceive and he'll make sure that nothing will be missing from this seduction. What do you love best, women, drugs, liquor? Whatever it is, that's what he will provide. As you enter, you might think that it's going to be a good time but it's your death sentence.

Luxurious hotels, many times are used as death houses for a potential King. Major casinos are attractive den for evil. We are never to be fooled by all the glamour when we are destined for greatness. That's one of the reasons we must stay humble. That high school sweet-heart, you just don't disrespect her because of pride, wealth or promotion. As we reached to the top of the ladder, let us remain humble because the strange Woman syndrome can be fatal! As Kings are led to these luxuries, the enemy is laying in the cut saying, " IF HE ONLY KNEW WHAT HE'S GETTING INTO!" and we men that are driven by attraction and power, are so often led easily, like a lamb to the slaughter not having an insight that our slaughter house might be just around the corner. We'd give full cooperation only to our own demise.

The flesh will get you killed man! On the count of a whorish woman, a man is brought for a slice of bread. Your value is reduced to nothing when the flesh is finish. How do you think great men fall? Not all the time by a man made weapon, a hand grenade, an M16 or the like. They are often caught up into luxury, trailing after the flesh, become greedy, being envious of the finest things in life, vanity, said the preacher! Murdered in the "limo," killed making huge transactions, fine jewelry sparkling, the diamond studs, killed exercising his gifts and talents, mauled over by great wolves. Overthrown because of his potential, they see from a distance his God given potential and the enemy made a wish list, put a bounty on his head.

The enemy is an awful beast my friend. When you thought that you will rise to the top, when you see a way out of poverty to climb the ladder of success a dart strikes at your heart. It's not strange, it happened to many, they were after David hard, only that

God had been the rock and his fortress all the time and nothing could touch the property, the anointed of God. Know you can't touch God's anointed because, a thousand shall fall at thy side and ten thousand at thy right hand, but it shall not come near you! No way, they'll fall powerless before you, baby!! Touch not mine anointed and do my prophets no harm, saith the Lord. Great talents, men of valor, have been snatched out from before us long before their time, prematurely! The Devil is a lair, you've seen with your own eyes all the funerals of wonderful sons, taken out, slipped away from us due to some stupidity, and we say, "why did he have to go so soon?" Something was going on which the enemy new, he was going to be a strong force to reckon with to tearing down Satan's domain, a warrior, powerhouse for God! The enemy couldn't afford that, he won't allow the King to be seated on his throne, because it will messed up his agenda. That son was going to sing some people out of their problems, dance some people back to life and lift some people out of their burdens and release some that are bound in their trespasses and sins by the power of the Most High God. Satan couldn't afford the King to come to maturity, he cuts him off before the time.

Remember those Great Kings in your family, and in the community how very brilliant they were, making things happen, now you have to visit them in prison. They were never destined to be a murderer, no! Not at all, they have a future that was destined for greatness. That son was never operating in the capacity of a thief, a rapist or a gang banger. As he begin to reflect his God given ability, Satan unleashed his poisonous venom that gets into the pipe line of his anointing and suddenly you begin to see the clusters in his attitude a blurred attitude. Your children that were ambitious and strong are now angry kids, and you wonder, "Where has this anger come from?" It came from the attack, he is so bitter that everything is a problem for him and it will only be the power of the Almighty God that can break those strong hold and release them back into their destiny.

You wonder why the Devil is so upset. A King is set to rise and the enemy cannot allow that his kingdom is threatened, thus at the very mentioned of your son, an unusual cloud of anger rose up in Satan's camp and now all kinds of assassination attempts are coming at the prospective king. Just when you least expect it calamity strikes! Did you hear who killed such and such? Did you hear who was killed last night? Oh yes, you can say all you want, we make the sad mistake of turning our backs on the Kings in our family when we see them acting differently. We do not stop to identify the root of their problem, why suddenly he's drinking so much? Why is he smoking and doing drugs'? The good boy that was raised in your house hold, suddenly drifted off into homosexuality, what is happening here? He's not interested in the things he was once motivated by, he withdrew from the family and isolated himself from every positive affair.

There's an undetected problem which must be dealt with, but it's so easy to turn our backs and blaming them for failing, oh it's just the company he keeps, oh it's just his bad choices. We make all the excuses we can find but fail to understand that the enemy was at work all along, slowly taking the energy away from him, in fact, stopping his ability to dream. Your sons, your brothers, your uncles and fathers did not just get to the place of total destruction by his own free will, the truth are hidden and he's screaming out for help! It wasn't his destiny, it wasn't designed that way from God! You knew them before, all along they were with you, yet you never noticed the difference. God didn't make them to be a failure, when he had imparted such great anointing on their life! The enemy couldn't kill some of them in the natural, because the Lord wouldn't allow that, and all the time Mr. Satan poured and poured to his demise, some kinds of sickness from some strange places which got hold of them, or they wound up in prison. But I still believe that what the enemy meant for evil, God still can turn it around for good, because he is God! Don't ever fail to realize the number of anointing and the number of "David's" that are locked away in some prison somewhere, but we sometimes with our "holy ghost" cannot see what the issues are. We blame them and cause even more pain to what the enemy has already inflicted on the ones we love. We even abandon, crucify and treat our wounded as though they are not worthy of a chance to recover. We've been blinded by our own ignorance and self-righteousness. If some great Kings survives in the streets as they search for help and answers, many times they get lost or misled by the cruel hands of the wicked, unfortunately our children can't run to just about anyone with their problems, due to the deceptions and the coldness of man's heart, so they struggle with their deep rooted issues until they end up joining the gangs, finally they wound up dying bloody in the streets.

The Kings need direction and when no one is available to them, they often drift into behaviors they adapt from other peers as they roam the streets looking for validation. Finally, they end up in the "pen," and as we are so shallow and naive with our views, we often believe that it's from his own self-indulgence, yet the enemy had been at work all along waiting for his moment.

Beloved, an army of satanic attacks are going after your son only because he is gifted. What? Just think about the gifts and talents which David possessed. A great musician, he played skillfully, played King Saul's sickness away, the man dances so well that he was actually despised by his wife, his wife just did not love to see him show out like that. David fought and prevailed against the giant, Goliath. This great son was loved by everyone and he was a beauty and charm to not just the family, but to the nation of Israel as a whole. Women shouted at David in admiration, "Saul gained his thousand, David his ten thousand, every woman wanted to just be in the company of this great son. He was very popular, even in the field caring for sheep, sheep were drawn to him, he was known for his anointing, this was evident because he believes in praising and worshipping God, the super natural power of God could not be hidden!

Anywhere that greatness lies, remember that death angels will labor long and hard in their attempt to abort a dream. They will not rest until they are satisfied with their destruction. We cannot, and must not, be ignorant about the enemy's devices. In fact, he is very brutal in his attacks against royalties, many are slain by him. Many are taken down by evils, thrown into prisons in a direct effort to stop them from dreaming.

Yet, by the grace and salvation that God has given, we've got to seek our sons, know where they are, know what they are doing, weep and pray over them, plea the blood of Jesus over their lives so that they can live. I know that by the divine power of God they can live and declare his glory.

A King in Rebellion

Chapter Nine

Why do great Kings fall into rebellion? Not because they are all together narrow-minded in their perception or that they may exercise poor judgment in their ability to lead God's people. In cases such as these, it is important that we look at their rebellion from the Spirit's prospective. The Bible said that rebellion is as witchcraft. Yes, rebellion is demonic, and, demonic strong holds are often times at the root core of every effort of attaining a level of spiritual success. There are spiritual wickedness which must be overcome that stands in the way of the righteous like a monument, and in one's zeal to prosper and accomplish greatness he can become blinded by the attacks that come against him.

It is a fact that a prospective King naturally believes in himself and what he is destined for. He also believes that all those around him held dearly his overall interest yet, unbeknown to the truth, they are surrounding him only as the set-up from hell! There are those that will watch and wait only to wreak havoc and causing strains and setbacks to all you try to accomplish. The enemy places his soldiers and all those he'll use to destroy you at a strategic post, so that whatever direction you take, there's an unknown weapon which is pointing squarely at you where you can neither run nor hide.

It is imperative that we that are pressing towards our destiny that we keep our spiritual eyes open to those that are especially close to our circles. Many people just want to be close to the King for recognition and they'll seek this at any cost, even at the expense of inflicting serious wounds to the cause strains and setbacks as they realize your mission. The closest associations can many times be used as serious weapon against us. For one, they can penetrate with greater force since they are more acquainted with your whereabouts. They are the ones that you trust the most and they'll sneak you like bear without warning. You spend all the time in the world trying to figure out what went wrong, not even having the slightest inclination that the "Monkey" is right in your nose, you've been kissing the monkey, feeding the monkey, dancing with the monkey, and even vacationing with the monkey, having a good time, not knowing there's a major problem within your camp.

Monkeys are very slick, but not too slick, they can be detected. The sad thing about these monkeys are, many times they are real dedicated to the cause as those that are sincere. If you're not good at filtering them out you are doomed! Angels in disguise, they are dependable, playing their roles quite well. This is the ideal plan that Satan uses as his strategic device to make you feel comfortable, then later at the right moment, he'll make his attack and, buoy, does that hurts? The pain felt from one that you've trusted only to find that he turns against you is very severe, it can cut deep. You know that the enemy is out to get you and you constantly look for the attack, but a trusted friend, you would never see it coming! That's why it's dangerous! An inner circle injury is so devastating. The same strategy one uses for a small target, it's not necessary to use for a big catch. You might need an army for some situations, yet, for others all you need is a naked woman. A man loses his mind and integrity seeing her naked. That's why we can never stop pleading the blood of Jesus over our children, so that their dreams can be a reality. Blood coverings are important and must be implemented and follow up as often as possible.

It seems like in the world today, there is a thick cloud of murderous venom spewing against our children to knock them off their God given anointing. The murderous spirit of Pharaoh is still at work in the world today, he is still concerned that a greater King, a more anointed King might dethrone him. We are even fighting a major Herodic spirit that remains prevalent in our society, especially in our schools and our communities that still wants to kill every first born sons. They are still following the stars, bringing with them many gifts that are really not true gifts. They are doing everything in their power to prevent these Kings from rising to the top, fearing their kingdom is about to be reduced to rubbish. The special anointing on your sons is not cheap, it is very costly, it comes with power and prestige, just observe the spirits presence how it draws wonderful individuals to your sons. People are so very attracted to the anointing, they saw it from a distance and embraced it.

In the journey of our lives we strive through the tussles and dark gloom and uncertainties, and we must fight with passion and conviction. We must fight if we are to soar like eagles. It is by fighting we are certain of who we are and who is actually fighting with us. Throughout David's life, many battles were fought and won, yet he was convinced that the

God of Heaven was always fighting with him else he were bound to fail. He went up against Goliath and prevailed, not by his own strength, he was confident that the Lord was with him. A true King is never born with the notion to quit, we fight today, coming back tomorrow to fight again and if we must fight the next day, well so be it. We are to be determine to protecting our God given abilities and will never allow anything to take it from us because we are true fighters, glory to God! A King having a set vision focuses on that vision and geographic location cannot be a deterrent having his goals in mind.

There are no bars to hold a dreamer, he never loses focus on his true identity. A King may not always live in a physical palace, yet, he is confident of who he is. A King must act different from everyone else around him, "royalty!" In his mind and spirit he dwells each day owning great palaces and living in a world filled with peace and tranquil. Having had his destiny in prospective, any given situations you might face, no matter what he throws in your face the diamond will still glows. Real diamonds are not cheap neither are they fake however, they are found in unusual places, you might have to dig deep, dig into trenches to scoop up certain quality of diamonds. Once you see where they are found, you will almost never imagine that its richness and beauty will be of such peculiarity. Yet, we must never forget either, that a seed must die for it to produce and multiply in abundance.

We still must consider that the God of the universe is still the resurrection and the life one who is still raising up Kings, especially those that have been through the roughest places of life. How God just knows how to clean them up, polish and shine them so that its perfect elegance can be displayed.

So many times we might see ourselves buried in the grave of our situation, like Lazarus, no one even care to see us in our condition, yet the Master walks by to see what's happening. "Master! Leave him alone, he must be stinking by now!" God will have compassion, you can count on the God of heaven even when found in the grave. The sad state that you find yourself in, even if the Savior wants to bring you back, there are those that wish they could dictate to the Lord, " please my Lord, just let him die. " People wish that Christ would join in their partiality and be their so called "yes man." Jesus is such a Savior that will not allow anyone to denying him entry to rescue any of his people. God will not say "no" on the command of those that are not in favor of your blessing. He said, "Don't worry! Don't you know who I am? I will put life into that body that was dead, you better not ever try to underestimate me. I will give you the biggest surprise of your life." Since I know what death is all about, remember I was dead too sometimes back, and they had even buried me yet, on the third day I arose from the dead. I didn't stay in the grave more than the time that I had wanted, only for three days and I arose, I burst that tomb and I rose up triumphantly.

I am still able to do the same thing for men that are dead. You better understand the person you are looking on, I walked down into hell and I snatched from Satan, the keys of death and hell, walked back out of hell and I proclaimed the truth to the world. "I am he that liveth, and was dead; and behold, I am alive for evermore, Amen; and have the keys of hell and of death."[19] Nothing is hard for the King of Kings to perform, all glory to God for that wonderful Easter Sunday morning! When Jesus burst the tomb, it was by the

---

[19] Revelation 1.18

power, like a dynamite, the power of the Holy Ghost! Jesus and that same resurrecting power is still flowing and it is still strong. Regardless of where one has been, I want them to know that I have been there too, I can identify with their suffering, I know what death feels like, that's why it's not hard for me to pull people of all race, color, or creed out of their sin so that they can have a new life. No place that you've found yourself are you left hopeless, there is hope, better hope in Jesus Christ. If people want to form an opinion or make an assumption of who you are, you know yourself better than anyone else.

The fact that you've made a mistake that in of itself doesn't define who you really are in the eyes of God. People are prone to make mistakes, a true fighter will not-stop fighting due to some accidental low blows, after you are knocked down in the ring of life, you can find the strength, the courage and the "where it all" to rise to the occasion and be the true champion that he created you to be. You can whether the storms and If after you get up you feel a bit weak and are unable to fight, the general rule is, "jab a little, jab a little," protecting your face, protecting your heart, shield your spirit. You are never a failure if you are willing to stand up and fight in the race of life. After David looked back on his accomplishments, he would conclude, "I have been young, and now am old; yet have I not seen the righteous forsaken, nor his seed begging bread."[20] God's divine power never seized to prevail when our determination to fight is rooted in the ability that the holy spirit fights alongside us.

---

[20] Psalms 37.25

A Gift in a Humble Fighter!

ஓ

Chapter Ten

Many people are misled believing that you must be radically violent to fight and win. I beg to differ, because I am told of a man named Joseph that had proved the opposite. As I concentrated on Joseph's horrific experience, it was a fight, the greatest fight of his life. He must be a genius winning this fight using his best battle plan, "running!" It is a convincing contrast between David and Joseph. We can all attest to the fact that everyone's test can never be of the same nature, neither are the effects the same.

I do believe that everyone has his own cross to carry and the fruits yielded from many of our trials will one day lead to a reward to the very people that thought less of us. Certainly, we must take up our cross and carry it with joy in our hearts. We realize God will never give us more than we can bear. The fact is very unfortunate, David has lost control, and fell for Bathsheba, which cost him a great deal. Yet more significantly, Joseph ran from Potiphar's wife and it too, had even cost him greatly. Not- wit- standing, however, his penalty was a blessing to him in the long run. David saw great pain and sufferings because he was unable to flee. On the contrary, when we look keenly on these two individuals, Joseph's integrity supersedes David's by a wide margin. Joseph was no doubt a man of unsearchable courage and character because he possesses the strong will to flee his attacker. No doubt that Potiphar's wife was presented as a beautiful woman, and no one would imagine she would throw herself on a Hebrew slave that was just working for her husband. She was blessed with all material necessities, yet, the heart was so sinful that her sexual cravings were burning to the extent that she will deprive even the humble of his dignity forcing him into sin.

The word of God has pointed out many times how God will make a way for the righteous to escape our trials and rightly so he did. The Bible said, "There is no temptation taken you but such as is common to man, but God is faithful who will not suffer you to be tempted above that he are able, but with the temptation also make a way to escape, that he may be able to bear it, wherefore my beloved, flee from idolatry." Beloved! Joseph could have fled this great test, David just could not! When we suffer for the cause of righteousness, it will pay off in the long run.

It is true that integrity speaks loudly and God is still looking for men of such character, here Joseph possesses that which God is looking for. When we stand up for righteousness, God will honor us, and at every cost will righteousness prevail. The man that loves God will not allow lust to be conceived in him causing him his life. I know it's a hard thing, but the kind of assassination attack which was directed at Joseph was not on a local scale. We must never undermine the kind of weapon that the enemy will send at us. These attacks are still destroying people with great potential. Yet, what we do with these propositions are really what matters.

Every time we are offered nice things, doesn't mean that we are to accept them if we want to live. When one is destined for greatness, the enemy will send attacks from every angle, and he will not only send them locally but he'll even use the elite to perfect his job if he must, in order to abort the prosperity of your destiny. He will unleash assaults, even from the palace. To tear you down.

The devil works even in the palace, he's at work in the white house, in the jail house as well. Certainly, there are no discrimination with him. When he's after you he'll use any strategy because his plans must come through by all means necessary. We cannot be ignorant of the devices of the devil, he is cunning, crafty and he'll fixed himself in a "Queenly" array only to get you killed. Satan already made the assessment of Joseph's potential after all. He was convinced Joseph would never be trapped by local confrontation, he was clever enough and had the ambition and destined towards greatness. It is true that minor problems are for minor people, while major problems are certainly for major people. When you are destined to be real major in the things of God, you will suffer at a major scale. Like Joseph, his problems were so major that it takes a God that specializes in major situations. That's why when God delivers one from something major, it baffles the mind, and the world around becomes amazed at his power. Do you serve a "major problem solving God," one that acts in a major way at his disposition? The God we serves loves blessing people that's been on the cross, that's been in the grave, those that's been in the dungeon. Are you facing a major problem right now? Watch out, God got you in a major way. Joseph was blessed beyond measure, one good thing about Joseph was, that he was never carnal in his nature, he was not driven by flesh.

A man that is destined to be great, cannot live constantly in the flesh. That will ultimately stop the anointing from flowing. In the Devil's government, an interruption coming from the palace, attached with power, which would have tripped Joseph to thread had he been living in the flesh, but thank God that he was sober minded and was walking in the spirit of God. This wasn't strange, however, most of Joseph's life he was constantly under attack by the enemy, so he knew that whatever he did in life, he must always look out for the enemy to show up.

Satan saw the potential in the Shepherd boy and desired to take him down. That's just how he plots to bringing down the people of God. Wherever he saw the special sons, he knew there was something very peculiar about them. Joseph was sold into slavery, and because greatness was evident by all means necessary he wants to kill him before it manifest. Joseph was that special son from birth and his father knew it, he saw it in him.

Can you see in your sons that same greatness that Jacob saw in his son Joseph? Whenever you become aware of what your son possess, be it known that you have a divine obligation to cover him with every bit of God's anointing, so that his life can be shielded from all Satanic attacks that will surely pointed at him. As you begin to observe, you'll soon discover that when greatness was appointed, attacks from every side was also appointed. Don't be fooled by the often troubled beginnings, it is what comes in the territory of a full fledge anointing. Trouble will follow the anointing in your children's life only to create stumbling block and strong hold for their future. It is true that when a child is blessed with great gifts and talents, jealousy is at the forefront as their natural gifts surfaces. Yes, Satan advances himself in the midst and he'll come in all shapes and sizes.

Remember as the power of God was over Joseph's young life, even in his household, jealousy was present and they made sure they sold him into slavery, attempted to kill him, and still the king will rise because God was with him.

When we look through the eyes of the spirit, we must never second guess what causes the many setbacks, and often problematic upheavals surrounding our sons. The greater the anointing, the greater the struggles, because principalities and powers of the air are upset. In order for you to scale the mountain high, there are hurdles of all kind. You must fight some lions and bears. However, as you begin to understand the nature of the fights, you'll see just how necessary they are for your divine destiny.

Every battle won, you realize the great power source at your disposal. How did you muster an approach to conquering those demons? It was the power of the anointing which came from the father himself that had caused you to triumph.

Challenges precedes your attained success and Moses could attest to this fact. After all this man should have been killed as an infant, he was disposed of into the river. Yet you can never stop the plan of God, when God says he must live, he's gone make sure that he lives! Because God said it, it is true and the forces of evil cannot prevail against God's divine will.

From a shaky beginning, or a humble beginning, from the poor house to the white house, from the river bed to the palace, from the manger to the universe sitting on the throne of Heaven, "highly exalted." We never should look too much on our starting line, the real focus should be on the way we finish.

The race is not for the swift, nor the battle for the strong but for those that endure to the end. What the enemy meant for evil, God turns it around for the good. Trials and tribulations will never be a death sentence, but in most cases it can be a true path towards your destiny. There are times in our lives when we must welcome our dark tunnels, facing them head on, going through them regardless of all that might seem like a setback, how it can turn out to be a set up from the enemy. Yet, God will cause a light to spring forth within, and you'll see that there is truly a God in heaven that is still working in the favor of the poor. We must never minimize God's channels that he uses to bless us. I know that imprisonment is the least places that one would contemplate God's divine intervention and acts of kindness. In fact, we would frown at the idea of facing a prison sentence that would turn out to be for God's glory. Anywhere we find ourselves, a breath of his nostril can breathe life in any of our given circumstances. One thing we can never forget doing, is to submit ourselves in God's control.

Here am I Lord, out here in the wilderness, speak your word like you've spoken to Moses. Remember in the experiences of Moses, how his relationship with God had gotten so close and intimate, that God saw in him the ability to deliver his people, due in part to his attitude in the wilderness. When found in the valley, the sound of God's voice should be the most audible, and in the valley God pronounced his blessing, a blessing that will never fade. Out of every tragic situation when heeded to God's call, he turns your life around for his glory!

As you look back at Moses account, a murder was committed, yet it did not prevent God from placing his spirit in his servant. The power of God operated through him for his glory.

It is true that a vessel willing to be used by God, can be transformed by the power of God, whose ability outweighs every power of this world. No conviction stops God's promotion.

Here was Moses, a wonderful son, brought up with wonderful principles, loving, tenderhearted, and humble and a giving spirit. He could have enjoyed some of the finest lifestyle, yet, refused them only to suffer with God's people. As the enemy looked, he saw him and noticed something very particular, so he made sure that he turned up his murderous attacks to take him out. Do you know that the enemy is after you because you are blessed, and he just can't stand knowing that you have such an anointing? If you ever notice the way some people who are agents of the enemy, they represent Satan to the fullest extent. Doesn't take much to identify them, the way they look at you and frown, and the way that they treat you as though you are inferior. The dragon, Satan is at work and he doesn't even care, doesn't discriminate, what home or family you belong to, he is always lurking in the dark waiting for the right moment to strike. He has a mission to carry out, and for that reason, he will not rest until you are finally overthrown. A good son, will never forget the plight, and the suffering of his people. Moses saw what was happening to the Hebrew people, and he got terribly upset. At times, when you see the people you love, those that are helpless being oppressed and are treated with disregard, that would be enough to ignite some level of anger in the heart because of the love and concerns. In this situation, Moses in an emotional range, like anyone else, loses control. Yes, one can become bitter for a moment! It just do not sit well in your spirit, it can happen to you, In fact, to anyone for that matter. Have you ever been used so much that you get to a place where you just can't take it anymore? You can't think straight? Good people feel that way many times, and, only for the grace of God we are not all in the Moses' condition. You can be in the richest household and just not satisfied as you witness the oppressive state of those that you love.

Wealth will not take away pain, especially the most hurtful ones. The truth is, God only has the remedy for a troubled heart, a heart that is sad and burdened down with cares and heartaches. God will be the only one that can wrap his arms around those that are feeling crushed. The only prescription at moments like these, are a simple touch from a loving God. We see that in so many parts of the scripture, people will go through insurmountable problems, they try everything and nothing works, yet they hear about the Lord! The God that heals, the God that touches a woman as she was plagued with a serious bleeding condition. As she touched the hem of Jesus' garment, she was immediately healed. What great power is in the God of the Universe, still he'll remove the stains like he did for Moses.

Moses could not take the pressures, and he identified with the sufferings and could not turn his back, "blood smells blood," the thing that God puts into us from birth, our heritage, our family speaks boldly. He saw an Egyptian killed a Hebrew, that's my people man! They disrespect my people, in his mind, how could he just ignore those barbaric act perpetrated on his people? God even said it in his word, "Defend the cause of the poor and the destitute." In the heat of the moment, my friend, without having the time for deliberation, having no counselors around, no advisor nearby, a pain stricken heart, unfortunately, he murdered the Egyptian and hid him in the sand. Was he a bad person? One is burned with anger, he will almost all the time conceive in him, a corrupt heart. Who knows the thoughts of a man but God, he's acquainted with every details and intent of the heart and he knows that we are dust.

Emotions, Emotions, Emotions! God creates emotions. At the time of a burning situation, it seems like the decision making process is shattered, and only God knows what will likely be the fruits of our actions under those circumstances. In the case of a King's child, his action can still be fatal none the less. A good person like Moses killed someone and hid him in the sand, think about it, where did that thought came from? He was never a murderer from birth, something happened which triggered such an outrage, which is hidden in all of us.

In life, it is true that good intention can in so many ways produce bad results and in most cases, yes, "bad things do happened to good people." As said, Moses could have enjoyed the most prosperous life living in the King's household, his future no doubt could be secure and if taken advantage, inherited the finest opportunities as the son of a King. His quality of life would added prestige and would be something any person would have coveted. For good conscience, Moses was never a bad guy as some may have assumed. We must realize that when the heart is burned with grief and despair even the finest, most humble person will act out of character. He was not the typical career criminal which would require the world to impose on him a stiff penalty. It really was sad that a life was taken to that extent yet, one must be reasonable, the man was caught into a tough spot. It is not strange that a King's son possesses in him the potential to be engulfed in rage. This is every human reaction when faces difficult circumstances. Let's never forget, a son is a son and regardless of the outcome of his future, he deserves mercy anyhow.

Unusual situations bring about unusual reactions. We know that the pain and guilt associated with a tragedy of this magnitude would be grievous, in part, especially committed by a person whose lived a good life, and who was not engraved in contentious and negative behavior. When something happen and the perpetrator is one that we would expect conducting himself in those acts, even though it is hard to accept, yet, we can say, well that was expected of him, the opposite in Moses' case he was the anointed of God!

In this world, we have people that would kill every day without the least worry. They eat, drink, and party looking at the slain as though nothing had happened. Others, just to create a slight infraction towards someone, would cause such a major setback for them and they would feel such emptiness and guilt for days and years. There are those without remorse. And the fact of the matter is, we must wonder at times are some humans, really human? Come on, let's think about it. A human life is snuffed out and some persons would act as though nothing significantly had happened. That's not the attitude one should have in the event of human suffering, a real human must act with compassion and be sympathetic to the human family.

Certainly this was a deep struggle for Moses as he was there hiding in the desert because in the lonely moments he's gotten the time to reflect and search his heart. This for a long time, when he ponders of the love for his people he also felt the burden of the family that grieved. You can face with situations such as Moses, yet as you go through the desert, trust in the God of Moses and he'll give you the peace that you need. God knows the pain and he understand the heart that cries out to him. Even then, you are still able to be used by God to deliver many out of their sin and oppressed state.

Why a Wilderness Experience is Necessary

☙

Chapter Eleven

In the hustle and bustles of life, as we race to the forefront trying to accumulate our success, the wilderness can be the channel through which we'll obtain the best result to attaining them. God will use the wilderness to slow us down, so we may by chance, focus our attention on the most wholesome and lasting things of life. In the wilderness, one can see God's creation in a light that would never dawned on him in his haste climbing the ladder of success.

First, when in the wilderness, we must examine our relationship with God and work hard so that the friendship we establish with him is the best. The best possible way for any friendship to grow strong, is by true commitment to communicate. In our spiritual deserts, we can develop strong friendship with God there, like Moses. When we are committed to share in open and sincere conversation with our friends, the potential for strong relationship is realistic.

Moses developed a close friendship with God in the wilderness as he converses with him.

He expresses to God his deep emotional pains, his deep regrets, his desires and earnest expectations, openness! Let your friend knows exactly what you are facing, let them know what are your hurts and joys and sorrows, then you will know if they are real. God proved to Moses how very real he was by sticking with him in all aspects of his struggles. In the words of God, it is clear that Moses fled from Pharaoh but he never fled from God. Though you might have fled from someone or something, you can't flee from God. It's best that you just run to him. Run into his embrace! Look what God did for Moses, he will do the same for you as you are going through your own experiences.

God was with Moses, and so he'll be with you as you go through whatever pit falls of this life. Here is the pay off, God places Moses on to the right path, he sat down by a well. There is something that is great about a well. Jesus was at a well in the New Testament when the woman of Samaria came there to draw water. At the well, she received the living water that the Master Jesus gives. When you are going through your wilderness experience, it's very important to find a well.

The Psalmist said, "Though the waters thereof roar and be troubled, though the mountains shake with the swelling thereof, there is a river, the streams whereof shall make glad the city of God. It might be right there at the "well" that the blessing of God is waiting for you. God is waiting at that "well" especially for you! A man going through his valley, yet, constantly trusting in God, often times God will send him to the "well." That was where God put Moses in the right direction. God sent him and there you will find the right connection, the priest family. The woman went there and she met Jesus! When you meet the Priest, his heart is not to turn you away empty.

When you offer your service, Jesus won't turn you away, the Priest said, "Call the man that he may eat bread!" While in the presence of the Priest, if you conduct yourself as the man of God that you are, the Priest will see that all your other needs are met. He will most likely offer you his daughter to marry! Do you need a wife? Well handle your business, get by the well! At the Well you are at the place to be connected into greatness. That's what God does for his people. He meets you at the well to give the living water, you will never thirst again. It shall be in you springing up! Spring up O' well within my soul, glory to God! You just can't afford to stand at the "Well" and do nothing.

You must make yourself useful. Show that you are capable of protecting. Show that you are responsible. Show some initiative, and be the leader that makes things happen. Moses! O Moses defends the Priest daughters, he help to feed the flock, you can't be lazy and expect to be blessed by God, the ladies standing there feeding the flock, you must show some love and concern for the girls. Today, boys are not like Moses, they let the girls do the work as they stand there waiting to be chosen. Girls should never chose a lazy boy. Moses puts work in for his! When you show that you are up to the task and, as the report of your good conduct reaches the Priest, then he'll be impressed by the words of his daughters, and God moves in his heart, give him one of your girls!" I love it how God appears to us in the wilderness of our lives.

How low can you be that God can't reach you'? He can touch you wherever you are, in the trenches, in the pit, in the fire and even in the floods. Here, Moses was at the backside of the desert, what? Yes the far away part of the desert, in hiding. It was at this place, that Moses came to the Mountain of God and the Lord appeared to him in a flame of fire.

The miraculous work of God's power, so wonderful to see, oh! Look, the bush is burning, who put fire there? Very strange, I'm out here all by myself, Yet, God, is right there in the dark corners with his son. A fire, and the bush was not consumed, it must be God! Trust me, you may not be able to look into the face of God, but you can look at the face of his glory! It's a great wonder in the desert, you'll have experiences that you marvel at the divine power of the Almighty.

In the desert you must look up, as you gazed into the Heaven's you beheld and wonder! God called Moses from the burning and he responds. In your sufferings, just listen, just be attentive, he's calling out your name, his voice might be so still that you must be attentive my friend! Don't think for a minute that he's not looking at you in the wilderness of your life, notice that nothing can hurt you, the enemy can't oppress you, for the presence of God is with you. Glory to God! As you walk through your wilderness, expect your assignment, God has an assignment for you there, it is a "GOD PRESERVING ASSIGNMENT!" They are prepared especially for you. How can you be prepared to deliver souls from their pitfalls and afflictions if you're not trained? It is vitally important for you to undergo the necessary deliverance training of souls for you to be effective and skilled in the duties you perform! The training and the endowment with the power of God's spirit is very vital so that you will be effective and thereby effectuate change.

You can deliver people only from what you have a firsthand knowledge of in order to be effective. Yes you can help, or be of some help to some that might be going through a crisis. When it all come to reality, it's those that have been to the bottom, that God had rescued, those that were caught up into the clutches of sin and when everyone gave up on them, thinking they were too far gone, suddenly God steps right in, " A quicker picker upper God." They will respect you more after seeing what the Lord has done, raising you up from the dungeons! There are important lessons to be learned from the wilderness experience, the same person that you're running from can be the same person that God is training you to send you back to deal with! Moses had ran away from Pharaoh and here God turns around sending Moses back to him. You can't be fearful of those people when God is the one directing you. God will equip you not only with power, but also his anointing as a shield and armor. God is saying, "Don't Worry, I AM sent me to you!" Someone might wonder, why is God so strange? Yes he does strange things because he is God. Pharaoh wanted to kill Moses and here God is sending him to his killer; God stops the mouth of lion, he quenches the fiery darts, he parted the red sea, he can prevent this attack and change the heart of the King, oh yes, the Kings heart is in the hands of the Lord.

So here God is saying, the first Moses was powerless before training, this Moses I am sending is the fully trained and anointed, filled to capacity with power, this is what the wilderness does, you are empowered! So many people rejects the very thought of a behind the desert experience, thinking they are better able to finding power in the city, they're looking in the big city Universities, you can't find it in Yale or Oxford, no! The level of God's power and anointing that the wilderness gives, you will never able to get in those fancy places of society. You'll went in dry and come out dry not having the courage to unravel the plans to the enemy, but watch for those that have been to_ the desert, they got some power because the Almighty God was right there with them! Don't even try to compare the Holy Ghost anointing with those fake anointing, they are nothing close! A Holy Ghost baptism, filled with the fire of God, can never be compared with man's intelligence or his limited power, it just don't work! When you are humbled before God and seek the anointing in your life, you will undoubtedly do exploits! I've seen education with no power, yet I've seen some folks that's been to the bottom, and how God raises them up, and oh, how they are wreaking havoc in the devil's domain, they are reclaiming lives for God! Taking back what the enemy has stolen.

Once you've been through some stuff, you've seen suffering, you've endured some hell, and you've crossed the very threshold of evil that folk's vision would have consumed you. Now by the grace of God, you can help someone else to get through. You won't have to run from Pharaoh anymore, you will face him and be bold, looking in his face as you demonstrates to him the effectiveness of the God of heaven all over your life.

I Am, sent me sir! The one that walked in hell and snatched the keys of death and hell from Satan, the one that liveth, that was dead and proclaim that He is alive forevermore, He sent me! Am here under the command of the one that said, let there be light and there was light, the one that thunders in the heavens, that's who sent me and I am not afraid, because all power is given unto him, I am coming in the strength of the Lord! I got some work to do Mr. Pharaoh, there are some people for me to deliver, and I must charge you with what the Lord tells me to say to you.

Even Kings must submit to the King of Kings! The Lion of the Tribe of Judah is in full operation, if you act up, "Mr." he's not afraid to destroy you! You see, when we really know the God that's fighting with us, a never "BACKING DOWN" God, Kings and power will fall powerless before him, because he speaks and calls his name through fire in a burning bush!

How dare you despised your wilderness experience, God has a way of turning things around for the good. You will make it through the rough time, remember that after every struggle, it's an opportunity for greater blessings. Stay in the fire and burn for a while! Why are you crying because it's hot? It's hot, but hush! Moses knew what God was capable of doing. If you don't believe that it's possible, ask him, he'll tell you.

The wilderness won't kill you friend, it's going to make you into a man that will deliver my people out of bondage. God uses the foolish things of the world to confound the wise. He's doing something new. As you go through, don't think of yourself as inferior to anyone, the transformation process is never easy. You're like diamond, you are special. How precious is a diamond in the desert? Even folks that once loved you they won't even acknowledge you in the desert. They thought less about you, but it's for a reason.

You don't need distractions on this your mission. It's true that some folks will only come in your life to bring discouragements, letting you feel more heavy and alone, but all you need sometimes is God.

When you're shut in with God and hearing from him, that's all you need. You don't need anybody to pamper you and to whine and sympathize with you in your desert, you got a pillar of cloud by day and a pillar of fire by night and sometimes that's all the support that you need. God leads you and guides you in the desert, and when you're thirst, he provides water in a rock. Although diseased and infectious insects and wild snakes are all around the desert, God will direct all your steps, and nothing will by any means hurt you. Get on living and enjoying your isolation, your rejection will truly worth it, never mind, it will be all right. When you get back to Pharaoh, he won't be able to deal with you, the anointing power of God will be too strong for him and you know that evil will not survive in the presence of the anointing.

It will be a Holy Ghost explosion when you step in front of wicked Pharaoh again! What a day it's going to be! Glory to God! You will not be empty, you're on an assignment. You're going back to Pharaoh. And not graduating from their typical university, not the famous military academy West Point, you don't need their qualifications, you don't need their strategy, and you have your "Master's Degree" from the University of the Desert, on the "Back of the "Desert Training Academy". The Holy Spirit taught you how to live holy and set apart.

The greatest Professor! Jesus Christ the Master Teacher was present as he administered on the subject of Endurance. The anointing that comes from the wilderness, is much better because coming out of the desert you understand how to be humble, how to suffer, how to love and how to appreciate what God is in your life. I wouldn't trade the degree from the desert for a Yale degree! If Jesus is involve that's all that matters! You are trained by the one that gives power.

The power of all Powers! You have obtained a Master's Degree from the Throne Room of a Super God, that's a power that Satan cannot destroy. When they see you, they won't recognize you, they will be looking long and hard, to really figure who you really are, for the anointing gives a new identity! You'll be so filled up, pumped up, and fired up, people won't really understand what is going on, what's making you so bold and courageous, it's the anointing!

Face the Enemy Head On!

Chapter Twelve

Now you're concern with the enemies that try to kill you, the one who forced you to flee into the wilderness? Look my friend, those enemies which had tried to kill you, I want you to just stay a while longer in hiding. God is keeping those folks over there under subjection, you don't have to worry about them, just get yourself together, and God will deal with those that want you dead. Yes, he has something for them, the bible said, "Touch not the Lord's anointed and do my prophet no harm! They will not lay a hand on you, the elect of God, the God that we are serving will not allow that.

So many people tend to undermine the ability to be productive as a student in the "International University of the Wilderness." They would pay thousands going to the famous and prestigious Universities, graduating from them, having the best kind of training, yet, they will never be able to achieve a victory over a King that pledged to assassinate them. They can never face the King because they are empty, they are educated, yet empty, they are powerless and the only source that can fill them, is to get in the program with God.

There is a power that comes from the throne room of God, it only comes through suffering, you must be able to go through and endure, and that's where the qualification come from. God's standard of training is superb, you can never find that anywhere else. God has strange ways in commanding his blessings and it's ironic that certain folks will frown at the idea of a man that God puts through his training. That's why they marvel and are bewildered, having seen the manifested works of God, because they have failed the test coming from their prestigious Universities. They must understand that God never fail when he's at work, his training is the one that gives ultimate results, a result that will last. The Bible said: "Behold, I have refined thee, but not with silver; I have chosen thee in the furnace of affliction."[21]

People's attitudes are strange due to their lack of knowledge and shallowness towards the wilderness. They shake like leaves at the thought they might be going through such an experience. O my God! I don't think that I'll last; I can't handle this, they make all kinds of excuses as though their very lives are coming to an end. We must realize that God will not take us in the desert to have us killed, he will make sure that we are protected in the desert. He'll meet our needs in the desert and he'll make certain that our shoes are securely strong, that they will last while we are in the desert! People of God, we must understand that we are supplied with a flow of endurance in the wilderness. You learn self-denial, you learn self-restraints and you learn to trust God in hopeless situations, you learn determination and most importantly, in the wilderness, you'll find out who you really are, and who really loves and cares for you.

---

[21] Isaiah 48.10

Have you noticed as you're going through your "desert-like" situations, some people will express their love to you only for the first day. Yet as they realizes that you must stay out in the desert for a while, you begin to observe how they start to pull back into isolation, they can't even struggle with you as you go through your pains, at least giving you some emotional support. It seems like they almost immediately thought less of you, like you've messed up so big and that lending you a hand would be too much to offer. There, they just leave you for dead!

Have you ever been to the bottom, and you realizes those you thought had loved you the most, are the ones who never stop by'? They never reach out! Doesn't it sound like the "good Samaritan story? The good Christian friends just left you for dead! They wouldn't care if you live or die, they stay at the side line making all kinds of negative comments, making judgments, and even joined with those that really have hated you all along. Many people have gotten so holy that as they see a struggling saint they begin to pronounce an additional sentence on you, wanting to unravel your pass, oh, he did so and so some time ago and this is why such and such is happening. Yes that's the way they are not knowing that all your pass are underneath the blood, they wouldn't even offer up a prayer on your behalf, worrying that you might be delivered. Am telling you of folks that will put their feet on your neck, you're supposed to stay down forever!

That's why David said, it's not my enemy that had done this, it was my equal, my acquaintance, we walked to the house of God in company, eat and live in the same house, share our clothing together and so on. They are the people who treat you unworthily, like nobodies, and a nothing! At times if you could see them, they're wishing, hoping earnestly that you are found dead in your wilderness.

Yet, God is with you at all times without a doubt and he'll pick you up and will himself carry you through the rough terrains of the desert. The same people that you've stood by through their storms, when they were going through their stuff, you were right there, but they abandoned you in your condition not knowing it was the power of God bringing for you a promotion, wilderness and pains are taking you to a higher place in God, only if they'd know just how much stronger you'll be as the pains are over. They just can't understand what you are going through, God's bridge to promotion, glory to God!

David said, "As for me, when they were sick, my clothing was sackcloth, I conduct myself as though he had been my friend or brother. I bowed down heavily as one that mourned for his mother. But in my adversity they rejoiced and mocked and have feast." We can't be discouraged at the way people treat us in our struggles. God, the God of Moses will walk right in the desert with you, feeding you with angel's food, giving you pure water from the rock, sheltering and protecting. The God of Moses is still alive and well, he is still at work in the lives of his people.

Using a Lie as a Lethal Weapon

Chapter Thirteen

Beloved, the power and effects of a lie can be severe, devastating, and in some case, detrimentally fatal. Lies are capable to cause major damage equally to, if not more disastrous as a military weapon existing in the world today. A lie has the potential of inflicting great wounds. The many wounded, the scars, the most extreme piercing and mental anguish that will pound your soul into oblivion should never be taken lightly. How deadly it is to be caught in the path of a "Hurricane?" These lies are very deadly and will sweep away those in its path. Yes, many wonderful people are slain daily by the effects of the poisons caused by them.

A lie aimed directly at the heart, when it strikes the blows are fatal, anyone standing in its way will be demolished emotionally, spiritually and it will take a life time of hard work to repair its effects. The Lord warns us not to bear false witness against our neighbor. We are constantly warned of the dangers of lying. Not just one's character will be assassinated, his reputation and credibility will be shattered, even to some degree, his eternal destiny, a hope of a life spent with Jesus can be so ruin once trust is broken, thus, reconciliation can become next to impossible.

In the book of Acts, lies have caused the death of Ananias and Sapphira. In this case however, their death stems from vows made which were broken. We see how important it is that we keep our word. They said that "word is bond," when we make a vow, it must be kept. Here they've made a pledge and at the time when it was required that they came forward, they held back portions of the money and this offense grieved the Holy Spirit, they died instantly. It is true that words uttered from our lips carry with it the capacity to seal one's fate that's why truth must be spoken by all accounts.

We can look at the situation which had transpired between Joseph and Potiphar's wife. It turns out that Joseph was blessed after all the mess she had put him through, yet, in many cases other's would be stuck for life seeking remedies and methods to resolve the unbearable damages due to the severity of the lies. An evil person can perfectly disguises his ills, and if we are not careful, precious souls with great potentials been wiped out before our eyes. Here was that humble, innocent lad, very handsome and blessed with a wide range of gifts and talents. The enemies saw this and pledged to use any means possible to destroy this young man. All Joseph wanted to do was to please his master to the best of his ability, nothing in him was actually pointing to sexual misconducts.

Looking at the Devil at work, he sends his master's wife with her sexual cravings only to trap this young man and to abort his destiny. She, like a lion in the jungle, preyed on the innocent, took disadvantage, using deceptions and her over powered abuse and sexual appetites. There is something great about a man that truly loves God and will walk in integrity. Joseph proved himself trust worthy and harbored no intention differing from his belief and personal convictions which he knew would affect his anointing. This young man was firmly committed to the duties laid out by his master Potiphar, and the truth is, not one part of his master's wife sexual agenda was part of his schedule. Joseph was very clear about this and would be very careful not to ever violate his God, or brought shame on his master.

This lady watched Joseph's every move thinking about ways in which she could seduce the poor guy. She would dress herself in the finest clothing, adding the best perfume and decking herself with expensive jewelry and make ups. One can just imagine her trickery, walking around young Joseph smiling and shaking herself, you know the deal, a major problem for a man! With all her efforts, Joseph would never accept her stuff. This got her very frustrated as time was actually running out on her, not willing to keep her evil schemes under control, she forcefully attacked poor Joseph as he was in the corner of the room. What's going on'? Joseph must have wondered in amazement. I can imagine the painful sight when this young man saw his hungry attacker. It is true that some women can really push the buttons only to take the weak through a pitfall and do anything to pull you into their mess.

Don't be fooled friends by the cunningness of Satan, the Devil uses even the master's wife though living in the palace to slay the people of God! When this happen, only the hands of The Almighty God himself will spare you because once associated with the Queen, most folks will not hesitate to make a direct plot at the poor as a mean to feel important in the presence of the Queens never mind her deceptions they will go as far as putting a blind eye to cover her sins. It is clear, most people associated with the Potiphar's will not think the poor is truthful anyway. Once her plans messes up she and all her confidant will accuse the poor making up a case against him and ultimately destroy his future, but thanks be to God, the God that Joseph serves is still alive today and is still committed to the defense of the poor. David said, "This poor man cries and the Lord heard him and deliver him out of all his troubles . . . O taste and see that the Lord is good: blessed is the man that trusteth in Him"[22] Even through a lie, a fight is necessary, in fact life itself is a constant fight to survive. You have to fight hard to sustain your marriage. You have to fight to maintain your family. You have to fight to survive on the job. You have to fight to stay healthy, stay holy, and to adjust to society's many changes. Fighting is important to stay in the race!

In the book of Proverbs Solomon said some very scary yet profound words: "By means of a whorish woman a man is brought to a piece of bread."[23] One can never imagine the many brothers that have over time became this piece of bread! You don't always have to be a bad person, or a whoremonger, or submit to society's standard to be classified as this piece of bread. It also includes the things we do for e.g., lowering our standards, sneaking in the dark, things that others would be surprised should they know about us! Did you know that such and such pastor is living a double life? Heck no! Not this stand-up guy, he's always doing the right things, in fact, in the day! Have you ever been brought to a piece of bread in your life time? Caught by surprise? It can happen, Oh yes it can! As you live your life in the best way possible, on the job, in school or anywhere you find yourself, an iniquitous woman will sometimes chase you down, and

---

[22] Psalms 34.6, 8
[23] Proverbs 6.26

as soon as she finds you; if you're not grounded, walking in the Spirit, you can be bought for cheap. You might as well call yourself, bread. Many people are caught by her deceptions at some of the most crucial moments. Have you ever been lonely, feeling down and out, having some very bad experiences? There it is, I don't feel to read the Word of God or even to pray, but someone attractive approach you, don't eat from that tree beloved, forbidden fruit is on that tree! Oh well, just this one time, you'll be fine, you'll feel much better! Hey brother, do you know what you are? W-O-N-D-E-R Bread!

The devil will bring before you things, and strange confrontations at the most delicate, the most sensitive time of your life. He just know the right time to make his move and he'll get you! I said before that he's subtle. The most striking thing about the book of Proverbs, the great wealth of wisdom and yes, it is also very scary, you will have to confront your own evils and look into your own back yard! Listen here, "But whoso committeth adultery with a woman, lacketh understanding: he that doeth it destroyeth his own soul. A wound and dishonour shall he get; and his reproach shall not be wiped away."[24]

"For jealousy is the rage of a man: therefore he will not spare in the day of vengeance. He will not regard any ransom, neither will he rest content, though thou givest many gifts,"[25] then when I look further I am yet baffled "For at the window of my house I looked through my casement, And beheld among the simple ones, I discerned among the youths, a young man void of understanding, Passing through the street near her corner; and he went the way to her house,

---

[24] Proverbs 6.32-34
[25] Proverbs 6.34-35

In the twilight, in the evening, in the black and dark night: And, behold, there met him a woman with the attire of an harlot, and subtil of heart. (She is loud and stubborn; her feet abide not in her house: Now is she without, now in the streets, and lieth in wait at every corner.)[26]

"So she caught him, and kissed him and with an impudent face said unto him, I have piece offerings with me; this day have I prayed my vows. Therefore came I forth to meet thee, diligently to seek thy face, and I have found thee. I have decked my bed with coverings of tapestry, with carved works with fine linen of Egypt. I have perfumed my bed with myrrh, aloes and cinnamon. Come, let us take our fill of love until the morning: let us solace ourselves with loves. For the goodman is not at home, he is gone a long journey: He hath taken a bag of money with him, and will come home at the day appointed.

"With her much fair speech, she caused him to yield, with the flattering of her lips, she forced him. He goeth after her straightway, as an ox goeth to the slaughter, or as a fool to the correction of the stocks; Till a dart strike through his liver; as a bird hasteth to the snare, and knoweth not that it is for his life. For she hath cast down many wounded: yea, many strong men have been slain by her. Her house is the way to hell, going down to the chambers of death."[27] If that's not scary then tell me folks, what would be! This is dangerous stuff, man! Wow!

There is a weapon, one of a mass destruction in nature that is scattered all over the world. They can be found at every corner, believe me, there are loads and loads of them at every turn. Simple truth is, you might not need to invade

---
[26] Proverbs 7.6-12
[27] Proverbs 7.13-25, 26-27

the "Middle East" in search of WMD'S, you pass them daily, in the east coast , hanging out up north, chilling out around west and going over to the south side, they are like bee. Mass destruction's unbeknown to many but are wide spread, they are placed there only to deceive, especially the men that are calling on the Lord. It is true that, a weapon is aimed directly at you, you might not see it, and it's disguised in a harlot's attire.

You can play the fool if you want, but, your only way of escape is to run to the cross, and run fast because if you smell her perfume you're in serious danger of getting trapped. Joseph understood this fact well, and he ran! Yes, he ran for his life, the man ran without his shirt! Foreseeing the danger and as a man of God destine for greatness couldn't hang around because this would have been detrimental to his faith and did not worth the risk!

Running will stop the power of the dart from striking at your liver. Why are they chasing after you? It's not so much that they're seeking pleasure, it's not so much that you are the only handsome young man around, it's the power of God that has given you that anointing and Satan has set up legions of his agents in the person of Potiphar's wifely images. They come at you in many shape and forms, they come at you pretending to be the most sincere, loving and kind individuals, even as the Christian sister, yet behind it all they are the angels of death, assassins! Watch out for them, don't let them sway you in their trap, their mouths are like butter, a holy buttery mouth!

The enemy will not stop short until he completely overthrow you, making mockery of your anointing, they see you, they are drawn to your anointing, in fact, it is contagious, you are the target, they speak to you the finest words even bringing you some of the nicest gifts, yet behind it all there is manipulation and deceit.

Have you ever seen someone with a very kind and sweet attitude, only to turn out to be devil in disguise? She's without warning! They'll do anything to get their foot into the door and once inside they make a turn for the worst! It's the way that Satan operates, presents himself as the Prince of the Air yet, like snake, you are bitten! Are you not given the spiritual, ability to discern? Then, why not use it, take off running!

The Bible says, we are to flee from the very appearance of evil. Is it too hard running from her beauty? Beauty can be very tricky, Potiphar's wife was the finest beauty that you could find, yet if you are walking in the spirit like Joseph, you will be able to see betrayal, deception and a lying spirit. We are to commend the brother for fleeing, for in the faces of beauty there's also a spirit of deception that is determined to take you to the grave. A man ought to be able to discern, that's viable as a protected shield for his anointing, and remembering that all that glitters is not gold.

Sometimes some of the best gold will not even glitter. This woman got everything in life that she needed to be happy, yet you see in this life, you can be the best husband, making all the provisions for your family only expecting that your wife would be faithful. Sin is such a danger, going so far as causing evil and the love and trust of the poor husband to be broken. She makes him feel so secure, that he's unaware that the wife he trusts is leading a double life.

Can you trust her simply because she's in the palace? No my friend, the strong hold of lustfulness are everywhere and this woman was entrenched in its clutches. In her craving for satisfaction she'll trap the very innocent, not only to destroy his vision but his salvation. As you look around day by day, you can see wounded men everywhere whose dreams and visions were superb, they have wonderful plans for the future and have made all the preparations needed to fulfill them, yet they make a very poor decision, refusing to flee when they should. You'd be so very surprised by the destructions that one mistake can create. It will mess up the entire fabric of your future.

When Mrs. Potiphar finds your son, he'll be wounded for life. I just wish that you could see it coming, but they're so careful to hide their important secrets. Can my brother's actually just live and be like Joseph? Can we find it in us to take off running? Only if we could keep our shirts loosed that we can run away if needs be. It's very dangerous when we know we must run but due to pride or arrogance we hang around and fall into the hands of a woman driven by lust. Hanging around, you'll likely inhale her perfume and you will never know the poisonous substance in its aroma that will trap you into sin. Once her perfume reaches the center of your heart you will yield to her offers of entrapment of the soul.

Have you ever gotten the smell of some strange perfume? That is stink, isn't it? You want to vomit because it is for a trap which your spirit rejects, if you hang around, too long you'll be staggering like a drunken man, by the time you regain consciousness you're already too far gone, drenched in her aroma of hell, you know that the effects are deadly.

You can see many wonderful men just going around in circles, confused and can't find their way home, people see them acting real strange and wondering what's wrong? What's wrong with my son? He was never acting like that before, you didn't know that he had gotten the opportunity to flee but he played the fool, now strange perfumes went into his system, he got slow poisoned and he needs help! You can help your son, it's not too late, call the boy and pump the poison out of him in the Name of Jesus! You can save him.

You must believe that if you make the right decision, nothing can stop your anointing. The attitude towards fleeing is not the norm in today's society, yet, to be safe and walk in victory we must step out of what is normal and just do what's right so God will be glorified in our lives. An aggressive woman, got a hold of Joseph's shirt, which was fine with the young man Joseph, she may have my shirt, but you will not have my salvation. I am not yielding to her seduction. It won't happen! She will not take me out like that, no way buddy, it's not happening! A child of God must preserve his salvation more than anything in this world.

Beloved, one thing that gets the devil mad is when his plots to devour fails. He gets so upset and restless, he quickly devises a plan "B" strategy which he'd thought would be workable. Mrs. Potiphar in her sexual assault attempts, as Joseph escaped her adulterous trap, got his shirt, now she was certainly upset, Oh, I don't believe that he rejects me, a woman that thought she is all that and more, to reject her means trouble! She will do anything to do you in, after she fixes herself up, puts on her make up and get herself ready for action only to be rejected, that's a problem my friend. This man's shirt now turns into a weapon against him, an evil evidence to destroy this man's future. If you run you're in trouble, if you stay, you're in trouble, yet the eyes of the Lord is still on the righteous and he will show himself strong on the behalf of his children.

This lady was furious, why are you so evil? You're playing a game and it back fired, now you want to act up, why? It's you that started all that trash, you initiated this, but the truth is all men are not "dogs" after all. Joseph was only running for his life, you're just sitting there devising a lie against the son of God. Liar, liar, your pants on fire! A liar will get burn for real, that's no joke, you lie on an innocent man, you will be burned, and that's just the simple truth.

Don't you know that a lying lip is abomination to the Lord? Well, your sexual appetites was never satisfied, in your shock and disbelief, you'll just lie on poor Joseph as pay back. Woman, what goes around, comes back around, you know that every dog has his day, pay back will come to you at some time or the other. When Satan is at work, he's truly working a devised plan of attack. "See you have brought in a Hebrew unto us to mock us, he come in unto me to lie with me and I cried with a loud voice. When he heard that I lifted up my voice and cried, he left his garment with me, and fled, thus she kept his garment until her husband came home." How damaging a liar can be'? Look how the poor can be slain by a simple lie? So many times you're telling the truth, but just because you are poor, the odds are stacked against you, you're not believable.

My wife will never lie, she is the mother of my beautiful children and she's a good mother, she'll never lie. Well, you're a liar! A man not expecting something that damaging from his wife will defend her and more often she's a devil in disguise. She cried and cried labeling the poor Joseph a serial rapist, oh, she's a serial liar! We've seen it in our society, regardless of the impeccable reputation and honesty of the accused, because of who the alleged victim is, you are still going down, no lie detector test, and you are still going down.

So Joseph innocently was thrown into prison on a false allegation, yet, you know who God blessed, let no man be cursed. The battle was not his, but God's.

Suffering for Righteousness

℘

Chapter Fourteen

Prison, for many, could be considered a death sentence to some estimation. Very importantly though, it can be the place where gifts and talents are discovered, a place of renewal or even a place of soul searching. In this life, most of our decisions are consisted of choice making. At every place in our life, we are cautioned to make wise choices, to this, even if you are found to be in prison we have a greater responsibility. Some imprisonments can mean an opportunity to discovering dreams, to become affiliated with hidden potentials, even to just pause, slowing down and let the Lord speak to us.

Often times, one cannot imagine the pains of imprisonment, especially those that lived all their lives in the palace. Yet, through the very act of pain, many are birthed with blessings beyond measure. Many times it seems so easy saying, "let's put him in prison and throw away the keys." An analogy used by those hurt or abused. It's easy throwing a poor soul into prison because you yourself may be able to buy or manipulate yourself out of the pen. For those that are guilty, it's almost always painful for one with a "soul," sending him to the pen. Many times people possessed with an evil intention when sending some into prison, yet as in the case of Joseph, his incarceration turns into one of the greatest blessing and we learn from his life, a choice maker!

Imagine a person that is really innocent, have tried his very best to live his life conducive to God's approval yet been thrown into prison. When a person is cautious of the way he conducts himself to protect his integrity and would never blatantly jeopardize his freedom, yet brutally and without remorse one would sanction his imprisonment knowing there is reasons to doubt his guilt is just plain out of order. What's wrong with the human heart of ours? Are we not conscious that there is a God to be reverenced, who is watching our every move?

Be it known that a righteous man will suffer for a righteous cause, yet, in his suffering, God will see him through. The point is clear, God said it and He is committed to honor the cause of the poor because he delights in the righteous. To suffer for righteousness, a man will be blessed because the eyes of the Lord are upon the righteous and even in the prisons his cause will be defended. In prison, even in the pen, as it is often called, the spirit of God was with Joseph, that's why we can all say to this one fact, "If God be for us, who can be against us." God will still prosper your ways, for if your ways please him, he'll make your enemy be confounded and be at peace with you. Yes it happened, God is still who he said he is! Have you ever been lied on, been wrongly accused? It's a terrible feeling, very disgusting. You know it didn't happen, you know deep in your heart, it's a lie, yet you can't even win, can't even defend yourself, no one wants to hear you out, no one thinks that you're worthy enough to believe.

Especially in today's world, money, fame and popularity is the order of the day. Society praises money than truth, they rather money over justice. In world of greed and gluttony, you are doomed if you are not politically connected and have people in high places, you are doomed! The young Joseph went to prison on the behest of a lying, out of control wife.

This same kind of mishaps still goes on in our community and around the globe, very prevalent act in our modern world. Yet, no doubt that Joseph was talking to God as this sentence was handed down on him, "Lord, let justice run down like a mighty stream," for the countless souls that are slain and oppressed by the stronghold of the wicked.

Will not the Lord arise and stand up and vindicate the poor out of the hands of them who is too strong for him? Yes, God will see you in the prison and his divine favor is on your life, there is great favor with God on your side for he will stand by the oppressed. You will not greatly be moved. Look what God will do if you'll remain faithful even in the midst of great trials, look what God will do even in the struggles, you can't loose with a big and mighty, most Powerful God of the universe. He's no respecter of persons, he will pick you up and establish you. He will make you the head and not the tail, you are above and not beneath. That's the God that Joseph serves because he rises to the top, and rises to the top and rises to the top!! Glory to God! He soars like the eagle, be patient in suffering, endure through suffering.

Is there anything too hard for God? Nothing! Though they slay me, yet will I trust him! You can never stop a dreamer, how dare you try to stop a man that has the divine favor of God? It's just not possible! God reveals himself in dreams and if a righteous man will dream, God will show him the greatness of his power, O yes he will! Joseph was excellent in his ability as an interpreter of dreams and God speaks through his interpreting. God will show forth his mysteries, what is to come and only those that he appoints will be able to explain them, that's why the King sought out Joseph for his ability.

The King needs you for your ability! In prison, not only his fellow prisoners sought him out, the very King which places him there eagerly wanted his service, when the King needs you, son, you are important. Remember that the ass was very important too.

Jesus, tell them, "I AM" needs him! Joseph was given the Kings personal ring and was promoted to the summit of political power, riding in the second chariot as the King, yes, from prison to second in command over the whole Kingdom. You can't touch God, son, God's ability to do, to act and to promote is just beyond our comprehension.

God's operation is divinely just and even the kings of the earth are and must submit to the King of Kings and Lord of Lords! The Bible says, "Before I formed thee in the belly I knew thee; and before thou camest forth out of the womb I sanctified thee, and I ordained thee a prophet."[28] The lies of Mrs. Potiphar can never impede the plans of God from coming to pass in his son's life, Oh no! It won't work. The power of God will penetrate lies and completely demolishing them, yes, lies are powerless before a powerful God.

Think about it, Joseph was directing the most populous Nation in the ancient world. How big is God? No weapon formed against you shall prosper, how big is the God that you are serving? How big and wide his vast domain, to try

---

[28] Jeremiah 1.5

to tell these lips can only start! A lie can be the door to your promotion, it can be your passport to greatness. A lie won't kill you if you can dream, the foundation of hell will shake when a righteous man dreams.

It is said that promotions come not from the east, nor from the west, but it comes from God! When God sees it fitting to promote you that's what he'll do, in fact, nothing and nobody can stop that! So you're going through something, so what? Keep going through, it means something, it means blessings, just see them working for the good as you're going through my friend. I feel good that the Kings heart is in the hand of God, it makes me feel real good, why? He will not do what God doesn't want him to do and he must submit to God's approval! Yes sir! God will turn his heart where he will, and his power is very limited when going against a "Super Power God!"

It is true that the anointing power of God will protect and shield, he will guide you, and nothing can by any means hurt you. Look, they meant that you will suffer, and rightly they were expecting to see that, but see, God turns it around for good, and now they are mad, "tell us why you're mad?" I say, why are you so mad? You're mad because you don't know the God that we serve, your mad because the God that you serve is a fake, he does not believe in forgiveness and redemption, your God is a fake, the real God knows that we are dust and he sends Jesus to be a Savior for us.

Your God is not Jesus, that's why justification to you means nothing! When you look at your sons, greatness lies within them, they are equipped with a capacity to be great, but as a dad, an uncle, a big brother, we are cautioned to give them the right instruction to flee! Don't let the danger surface itself first, we are to see it before it comes and flee! Don't let your sons expose themselves to the evils of Mrs. Potiphar, she is about your destruction to abort your Kingly potential, if they refuse to. You must go and drag them, pull them and if possible, don't leave them an inch, do whatever you can to rescue them. Mrs. Potiphar will not rest until she gets the upper hand on your son and she will poison him, you can't afford to stand around and allow her to create that trap anymore, she's a dangerous woman, she wears the perfumes of death.

It must be understood that through it all, God is still raising up wounded men, lifting them up, placing them into greatness to go out on mission for his glory. He wants you to feed the hungry, help the homeless, touch lives and give hope to the hopeless. Don't stay in your wounded state, leave your shirts and flee, it's "Cool," it's better to flee without your shirt than to ravish in her lust. If you do, you'll be cut off, annihilated, get out! Bounce! Vamoose! She's not worth it.

The Devil Will Give The Idle Work to Do

෪

Chapter Fifteen

If we claimed we are men of God, we must be busy at work for him, we cannot and must not waste God's precious time. We are called by God, not to be idle, the Devil will give every idle person some level of work to perform for him. That dragon, Satan, after he witnessed the anointing of God on your life, but you are constantly wasting your time dibble dabbling in things that do not please God. He is certainly going to make it his duty to put you to work. The danger is, the work he will give you, will not be something that you will appreciate, his plan is to feed you to the dogs, creating for you a life of confusion and chaos.

We are called into the Kingdom of God to build, and the truth is an idle King, can only destroy the Kingdom and ultimately destroying himself. Nothing can be more dangerous than an idle King, an idle leader, an idle pastor or even a Father or Son wasting and taking disadvantage, abusing God's precious time and resources. The Devil loves an idle official because he can gain a foot hold on his life. Until the time he realizes it, his energies and spiritual substances are drained by the devil's infested ruin.

David which knew better, could never see it coming because an idle mind can never foresees the danger. It creates an entrance to sin, and those who purposely live in a state of idleness can pay a costly price. Whenever you are called to be somewhere, but instead taking time away from that obligation, you are giving the devil a clear path to destroying your future. What are you doing in Brooklyn when the Lord clearly gave you an assignment in Albany? You are clearly off course and must immediately get back on the "Express!" David knew that he was supposed to be at the camp, yet he found time to be on the roof, which was way off course, your GPS not working!

Imagine if we could somehow spot from a distant the many traps set up by the enemy scheming, waiting for the right moment to attack. He stays in the dark determine to expose our weaknesses to the world? We are to watch out for those little unchecked issues, those look but don't touch issues, the little white lies, touchy feely stuff! It's the little stuff that are dangerous! The Bible says: "The woman was very beautiful," a very desirous kind of beauty, you can look through the comer of your eyes, no one will see you! The Bible said, "When lust hath conceived, it bringeth forth sin."[29] An imagination, OMG! Many times, try as you may to resist the temptations in your own strength, especially watching her taking a shower, beloved! You need the strength of God so you'll be empower with an attitude to flee!

---

[29] James 1.15

What an extremely beautiful picture created in your mind, if you know what I mean, nowhere is a woman more pretty than in the shower. Hello!

A man of God will ponder upon that image all day, and the interruptions in his mind can be overly devastating. We know that beauty is a good thing, yet not every good thing is actually good, some good things are too good and will turn into pain and problems.

Great Kings are ruined, not only by military powers, but by the deceit of her beauty. "Irresistible beauty." David could never be still in the evening tide, like most men they cannot think straight in the evenings. David couldn't resist, he sent to find out, "what's up?" He was dangerously curious! My God!" The Lord is my Shepherd I see what I want."

Something captures his imagination and got him to be completely restless, and I just can't help myself right now, I must get her! The danger after all was, he found out that she was the wife of someone else, someone in his own military, who was out in the jungle fighting his war. Yet that didn't matter anyway, for the sin was already conceived, it was growing full force, and once sin has taken root, it has no conscience whatever. It didn't matter at all, when David found out that the woman was Uriah's wife. She was very attractive, and she suits his lustful desires, not knowing this sin will take him too far and will ultimately cost him too much. In fact, if David was functioning in the righteousness of God as he knew so well to do, he would be more careful and practice self-restraint. But, you become blinded by sin whenever it's budding and began to bloom in your life. All it takes is just one slip.

Have you now realizes how easily the man of God can defiled his temple? A very awful place to be laying with the wife of another man. He knew the Lord was against adultery, he knew the dangers of taking fire into his own bosom. You can never over look this danger as a man of God, this will ruin your eternal destiny. David, what are you doing son? You were made for greatness! Bathsheba was not an idle, she was just doing the best thing, that most women adores caring for her hygiene, she was a clean and descent woman after all.

Look at the chain reaction, the effects of sin, a cursed generation, an entire life of misery. The woman conceived, now a child born from David's repulsive behavior, wreaking havoc forever.

Most of the time we find that the reason for our miseries are that we have made some poor decisions in our pass, then over time they resulted into a whole existence of pain that is so bad it trickles down into one generation after another.

Adding to the dangers though your sins are forgiven, the stains of your evils left a permanent scar that only the anointing power of God can erase. Are we glad, that regardless of how far the Devil may have taken us into ruin, we are still under the umbrella of grace? Grace will find us in the gutters, in the web, and even the children born under those very unfortunate circumstances, God's mercy still covers them none the less. God is faithful, oh yes he is!

None can deny David's unyielding love for God, he proclaimed in the Psalmist, "this poor man cried and the Lord heard him and delivered him out of all his troubles." When the righteous cries out to the God of heaven, he heats and responds. That is the assurance that we have as his people! The God of heaven backs up his people even in the down times of our lives. What a Mighty God He is'? Oh He's awesome! God knew His servant David before He called him in the field as he was carefully feeding the sheep, He understood David's heart and new that all men hold in themselves the capacity to sin.

How sin can attack the best of saints, really it lies at the doorstep of a human soul. It is true that Satan will surprise us with a visit, and by the time we realize the person we're entertaining it's too late, the lifetime damage had already been done. No matter who you are my friends, a man will lie at times to cover his sin! Looking at all David's accomplishments, we marvel at the thought that this same man whom God uses in such power and might, this same man was very able to be a compulsive liar, murderer, adulterer and so much more. Though he's anointed, yet possesses the sin nature, it comes from his father Adam! The greatest king that was ever known to Israel, a greatness which supersedes every other king of his day was known as a "man of war and bloodshed. " David's desire to build a house for the Lord sets the stage for one of the key passages, in scriptures relating to the coming Messiah.

God's message through Nathan is called the Davidic Covenant which is an expansion and a clarification of God's promises to Abraham. It is also an unconditional promise to David, that he would be the father of an everlasting kingdom. We can also add to the fact, David's first undertaking after being crowned King over all Israel was to conquer the city of Jerusalem and have countless sons and daughters born to him. David talked of his sons to be ruler, and reigned over Israel, as he conquered the Moabites which became his servants. David smote Hadadezer, king of Zobah, taking away thousands of chariots, and horse men, and footmen in great number.

When the evil spirit was upon Saul, we remembered that it was David that took the harp and played with his hand, so Saul was refreshed and was well, thus the evil spirit departed from him. Even though Saul gave David enough reasons not to fight Goliath, yet, the spirit of God which had laid strong upon the young man he was unstopped. David gave Saul the account of how he himself was attacked by a lion and how he caught him by the beard and smote him and slew him by his own hand.

This David was a no nonsense kind of guy, Mohammed Ali was nothing close to this great man. He declares, thy servant slew both the lion and the bear and that's the way the old uncircumcised Philistine would go down. If you violate the army of God, you will undoubtedly have to deal with David, you say you're a gangster, no! David was the man for real. He took up the challenge to fight with that giant, and David prevailed against him, taking him down by the power of God, that big old giant was floored and David uses his own sword to take his head off. After the Philistines saw what had happened to their champion, they were shocked and got to running, can you imagine?

Other great events of this great man of God, David later marries Saul's daughter, and the fame of the man was increased throughout Israel. David experiences many set-backs on the other hand, as jealousy crept in, his father-in-law King Saul plotted to kill him. You know that when the power of God is flowing through a vessel, someone wants to take you out! That's not unusual, it's here to stay! Yet you can't touch the anointed of God unless he allows it. Every attempt to take out David, he escaped by the grace of God.

You know the bible said, "a thousand shall fall at thy side and ten thousand at thy right hand, but it shall not come nigh thee." David established his army, the greatest ever in Israel.

He rescued the nation of Keilah, even got King Saul at a proper place where he could killed him, yet, allowed him to live respecting the servant of God. David fought and prevailed against the Amalekites, he captured cities and towns a list that goes on and on. His reputation was superb, a man so loved by all, people wanted to idolize him for all his gifts and talents along with his uniqueness and ability to accomplishing his tasks. Owning all these wonderful accolades, and to be at the place of power and prestige, those repertoire and sophistication could never have prevented him from engaging into acts of evil because the issue with sin is deep rooted.

It is clear that you can never purchase integrity, you can be the most prudent individual in this life. At a time you least expect, you are faced with a reality check, what kind of character are you made of. It's always good that we don't look down on the next man when he exposes himself. The truth is, all men are made with that part in us that just blunders, and then we feel sorry for ourselves later. You know it's true! Never act as though you've arrived. You're a liar holding that thought! A banana peel can knock you down, mighty men after all are never so mighty. We all need the Lord. Look at it my friend, David who had just conquered the Syrians, killing forty thousand horse men and it was recorded that everything which he sets out to do, God had blessed.

With all those wonderful blessings attributed to him, this same man of God would later became trapped, overtaken in a worst dilemma of the century. Not only that, the great

King went on into a string of lies and a slew of conspiracy tactics. A righteous king uses his authority to protecting his reputation on the behest of having his own faithful comrade dying brutally. That is very awful when thought about it my friend, what would have been the outcome of his indictment? He tried to cover up his dirt by causing the death of a faithful soldier, a husband. Is the blood of Uriah crying out as we speak?

When we try to cover up our sins, we do so by digging ourselves deeper and deeper into a bigger hole, but thank God for his great prophet, who will come and show us that we just cannot lie in the presence of the Holy Ghost because there will be consequence. He will expose us and we will be brought to shame and brought to our knees. I know that we must at times be looking at this situation as if David is by himself or was he really a bad person? Was he even that evil as some may even portray? No! See, what will you do in the event of justifying your sins? Most of us in our life time pays for the expenses of an abortion, or you may have hired a hit man, burned the house down. This was David's dirty laundry, he sends for the husband, Uriah, trying to force him to go to his house and lay with his wife. He wanted to give this man a bastard, you mean taking this man from the battle field and sending him to sleep with his wife?

Something just doesn't sit well here, the brother refused. He tried a plan "B" method, getting him stoned with liquor, he gave him a party, you know once you start drinking you get that sexual urges. David trying to give him a good time. That didn't work either. David am drunk but am not a fool, he went and slept with the servants at the Kings door. In essence, am not going out of the Kings sight. Uriah decided not to even leave the King's premises, he was saying here, just in case the king might think I went down for a "quickie" with my wife, I'm making sure he's aware of my presence, I want to be blameless! The King must have gotten frustrated, as every attempt to cover up were now falling apart. David went back and did some planning. Since this man will not cooperate, I'm left with no other choice, David thought about it, "I'll have to kill this man because all my stuff will leak to the public."

David devised a plan, he sent Uriah back to the battle field bringing with him a letter sealed and signed by his own hand, an executive order from the Commander in Chief, ordering that the General should put him at the heat of the battle so that he could be killed. Not knowing this plot, he took the letter as was told by the King. Without notice the General did as was instructed and Uriah was murdered in cold blood.

Sin can be so deadly, when the enemy comes into the life of an individual, no matter who it might be, it can be very fetal. You got the wrong idea if you think that Bin Laden and others such as him are the main people that are able to creating evil acts. The man of God can be just as evil especially when he is set off by an evil beast, the devil. Where did all these evil intentions come from? It was nothing that David had practiced all his life, in fact the opposite, all David new was worship and praise. One might fear the Lord greatly yet, if you are not always guarded by the Holy Spirit you are left to be controlled by a cruel enemy.

The enemy will have you using your status to commit murder, befriending your potential victim, throwing him a party, am doing you a favor, "go sleep at home with your wife." David called the man, I'm your friend, I like you very much, trust me, trust my judgment, how is the situation with the war going'? Everybody's living up to their expectation?

Is Joab making any progress? All these "Con" games. You know this young man Uriah must be saying, "What is this King up to? All kinds of thoughts and ideas must have been going through his mind. Can you imagine, you and this King never had a friendship going on, never had a deal, but the enemy in charge will make you want to soften your victim! You just can't afford to get caught out there like that. I agree that most soldiers would welcome this idea, going to spend the night with my wife, after all it's been quite a long time we haven't had some fun. Not even questioning the motives of the King, some of us would just jump on the idea.

We must check things out before we accept sweet offers! Something is behind a sweet offer that will haunt us forever! On the other hand, our own games can catch up to us! Yes, it happened! You did that before, come on, let's be real! Lying through your teeth, putting on the biggest front, "Go down to thy house and wash thy feet," What? Wash my feet? This man, I can imagine, must have been carefully analyzing this game, and to him, something just did not sit well. He saw David's too nice attitude, you know how we do it, fella's? Lay down our game plans, putting on the game face, trying to be cool with it. See a guy come up to you, you knew him but you're not cool, only an acquaintance, never communicated to that extent, suddenly he wants to invite you to dinner, he hardly knows your name yet calling you over for a drink.

What in the world is going on here? There are many reasons to become suspicious, did your mama raised a fool? Uriah was not stupid, he was checking things out. He said, "I'm not going down to my house! This is what integrity does, it's not right to go and have fun while the rest of my comrades are out there fighting a war, I'd rather to be with my battalion. This is serious business, its war time and not fun time, there's a time for everything under the sun. I'm in a war mood! When we think for the welfare of others, it is a good soldiering attitude.

If the war's not over and all my fellow men will go and have sex, then I don't think I should either. Why have pleasure all by myself when all my men are in pain? Selfish! That's clear idle, I'm better than that "Mr. King", that's just been thinking in the flesh since many lives have been killed in battle. When there is war, your flesh must be under subjection, you got to give your flesh a check every now and then!

When we think as a team we win as a team! In our selfish thinking, we will claim children that we are not even their fathers, that's serious business, you know that? Yes, it will happen! You just got tricked, pal! Sorry! You are so selfish that you can't even detect that the meat you are eating is poisonous, but you want to eat by yourself, don't let the King pamper you into believing that you are special, only to find out that you own his babies! No paternity test for you, look the baby doesn't even look like you. No family resemblance, He acts differently, nothing in common, you know this means trouble. Some of us just love to be pampered by the King, thinking that you are special, the king is up to no good, do you know of a no good king? It's so important that we seek to be even wiser than the King himself. You must check the King out because he can be looking at your wife acting as though he's just friendly. Don't let the King get too close to your wife, they can harbor evil intentions, lusting after what is yours. Hay King! That's my wife! What's up'? I will respect the King, I'll give him all the honor that he deserves but, my wife we won't share sir, no! We are not sharing my wife, my wife will not be our wife, Your Highness!

No one else is to be blamed but the King, God entrusted people into your care and you abused them, you shouldn't do that, you will pay! Persuasion, manipulation, cover ups, that's abusing your authority. Then once you're expose, you went even further, committing murder, conspiracy, crime of grave proportion, one thousand years in the maximum penitentiary.

That's what his sentence would look like in today's court of law. The truth is, Bathsheba might have never given in to David's sex crave, had it not been for the fact that he was the King. She understood how disastrous it could be, rejecting a King. In those days, a King's orders were to be followed under any circumstances, and especially a woman had very limited rights then. Can you just imagine had she said: "No, I will not talk to the King out of the presence of my husband." King David might have become furious and ordered her killed. So, in her mind I supposed, let me comply with the King if I want to live. That's the most logical explanation a woman could give under that situation.

In our society today, we can say all we want to, but, what else can we expect a poor woman without status standing in front of a King to do? She shivered into consent, well, Your Highness, is that what you need sir? O King live forever! Many times a woman are forced into situations she can almost never able to reject certain advances made by her employer, she may fears retaliation and unnecessary harassment or even threats of been fired. Often times too, she fear of becoming homeless or lose certain benefits. In the real world some women suffer very serious consequences standing for good principles, in a men dominating society they are quick denying women certain rights. In her convictions as seen before, that men will review and make decisions detrimental to her future, ruling against her, not to cause their male counterparts any discredit.

The world they say is not level and the truth is in the work place, it's not always the pastor who is your boss. Though many times even the ministers you've trusted are the ones come to be the dangerous culprits. They'll take sides even ruling against the truth, giving unjust decisions. Yet you must remain a true fighter, it doesn't stop even in the face of injustice, God will fight with and for you in his time. You've seen injustice how it ravishes your communities and even whacking havoc in your church. Men are naturally manipulators and at certain times they will not rule unfavorably against their brothers. They know that one day they too will fall and need that same dirty favor looking out for each other.

It is true that many people will go a little further engaging in what might seem as a small sin. Sleeping with him only to keep a job? Some may say it's a good thing. Others will completely reject that thought. In the competing world now-a-days, it seem like people will do anything to stay in the grind even at the cost denying their salvation. We must realize that God is not into the business of compromise. He requires complete faithfulness. Understanding that he'll never compromise on his terms of blessing us. When he blesses his children, he does so without restraint.

The Example of Struggles

Chapter Sixteen

Someone once said, don't waste time grieving. "Organize" Grieving will not solve the many problems and issues of life, Just organize, Things can turn out better.

Could somebody please tell me what was the driving force behind the Apostle Paul whose tenacity to fight in God's Kingdom was superb? He was a fighter at its best! Paul's motivation to fight, driven by his unyielding zeal to win, he was possessed with uncanny ability to stand under extreme pressures refuses to bowing out because of his faith in the Rock of his salvation. It is clear that when the power of God touches a man's life, everything about him will propel beyond the normal range. Because God's power is in operation and the supernatural forces of glory exudes his natural ability and the Holy Spirit will be the one governing his life that what so ever he touches they will radiate power from on high!

Looking briefly on the life of the Apostle Paul before his conversion, we can clearly observe how his zeal and motivation was rooted at the very core to destroying

Christians. This man had a very low tolerance towards Christians and would do anything to put them away because he was possessed by the power of the Prince of the Air. He was driven by an evil force. On a bright sunny day however, this man had a personal encounter with the force that is above all the forces of the world. That encounter completely overpowered the natural man, and replaced by the supernatural, changed his life forever. Today many lives are still changing because of that same transforming power of God! Paul's transformation was not just the ordinary one, it was in fact extra ordinary in nature! Only the power of God is able to cause an instant change in the life of a man so filled with scorn, mired in revenge and evil.

The fact is still true today that the natural man can only do as much as his limited ability will allow. To do great exploits in the fullest extent, those things that will be of an impact, it will take the supernatural anointing from God to make that possible. God must knock you down in your track and completely stripping you of your own self destructing will and your self-indulgences. God will have to place you at the pinnacle of your wits end, then when you become completely empty of the, "you like syndrome" that has been infesting your anointing, he then pours himself in that vessel and oh! No one that is functioning in the flesh will be able to comprehend with certainty what is happening, they began to wonder, is he losing his mind? That's just how deep the surgical power of God is, either you feel like you're dead, insane or you're stricken blind!

Unless you've been to your Wits end and God himself does the outpouring in you, would you be able to comprehend what the brand knew anointing is really about. Paul was never the same again, a new motivation, a new zeal to inspire greatness, a heart to conquer the enemy and visions to overcoming the wiles of the devil.

When making mention of the wonderful brother Paul, what are some of his identities: do we actually know much about him beside his radical side? Although he was transformed by the power of God, we remember that he was that vicious, murderous, torturous and brutal attacker against the people of God.

His ambition was to completely annihilate those that desire to follow the Lord Jesus Christ in true Discipleship. Before this wonderful conversion, he went by the name Saul, anyone that was familiar with this man knew how very dangerous he was.

This Saul as he was famously called, though he was deemed dangerous, was also very brilliant. It is said that Paul began his career as a fanatical enemy of Christianity. He would beat and imprison the Christians of that day, putting them through the most painful experiences he could. Paul started out with great status, highly educated. Historically, Paul was born a roman citizen which was very privileged for a Jew at that time.

This man Paul was also a great writer of Greek and exceptionally excellent in secular literature. In fact, Paul saw himself as a devoted Jew. Paul started theology in Jerusalem under the famous rabbi Gamaliel. Over time, Paul joined the campaign to arrest, imprison and execute Christians only due to his personal belief that these people were blaspheming God, saying indeed, they worshipped man and not God. It would be quite an experience for Paul having his time enslaving God's people, yet as he was creating mayhem, never understood the power of the most High God, who was able to call men out of sin.

On his way to Damascus to wreak havoc, there Jesus our Lord, who is master of all and is still speaking even through the clouds, called the man "Saul." In fact, Saul was still angry and speaking out terribly against God's people. He went into the synagogues seeking permission from the priest to imprison them in Jerusalem. This man was driven by the murderous venom of hell, he wanted everyone's life to be miserable, yet something significant happened in the offset. The Bible said, a bright light from the Heaven's flashed all around him. The power of God brought him to the ground and Jesus spoke to him in the best way that the Master could speak. He said: "Saul, Saul, why persecutest thou me?"[30] What a great shock Saul? Since you've been a trouble maker for quite sometimes, but here it was God's plan that you can never interrupt. In fear, Saul replied, who art thou Lord? Yes, he said "Lord." When you hear this voice, it's very hard not to recognize who it was that was actually speaking. Saul immediately was compelled to acknowledge him as Lord.

Jesus' voice was not just the ordinary voice, this was clear and distinct. It was holy! Even rascals can determine the voice of the master. Who art thou Lord? Saul, this is serious business! I am Jesus whom thou persecutest, it is hard for thee to kick against the pricks. You see when a man is driven by criminality, a man that breathes threats, and slaughters the people of God. When that person comes face to face with Jesus Christ he begins to tremble in astonishment. He suddenly starts shaking, oh he got seriously confused. The bad man asked, what will thou have me to do? Lord I want you to tell me, I know it is you, I am very convince, tell me what you want me to do Lord? So the

---

[30] Acts 9.4

Lord, my Lord and master, Jesus gave to him the stern instructions.

You can never underestimate the power of God, he speaks from the very element of the world, and even those that do not know him stand speechless. Hearing the voice, but seeing no man, that's just breath taking! What kind of great, big, Mighty God is this? With this powerful experience, Saul still was dumb founded, he needed assistance and was now rubbing his eyes, as he slowly stood up looking around wondering where the voice was coming from.

It is true that having obtained a real encounter with Jesus, one will never be the same. Saul was without sight for three days, there is something special about the number three. You might be amazed at the powerful anointing that one can obtain in three days. Remember that on the third day Jesus rose from the dead. Jesus said, destroy this temple and in three days I will raise it up.[31] Jonah was in the belly of the whale for three days.

The threefold cord that is spoken of in the word of God,[32] is not easily broken. Jesus had in his inner circle three of his disciples at all times, Peter James and John. If you want the anointing of God, there is something special about staying in the fire for three days! Saul couldn't see, eat or drink, the anointing of God will force you to a mighty three days of fast, man, that's the power of God in full effect! Saul, you are too dangerous, I must strip you down, come down off your high horse my son, I need to use you, but not in that boastful state that you are in.

---

[31] John 2.19
[32] Ecclesiastes 4.12

The Lord must humble you in order that you will be effective. The process of being humbled is uncomfortable and painful, you might have to lose those things that are dearest to you for three days. You know how it is, we are very stubborn, we are a stiff-necked people and it takes God and the powerful touch of his hands to come and straighten us out so that we can know with all certainty that the Lord is in total control of your lives. See, Mr. Saul, I'm not gone kill you, I just have to break you down, I just want your attention, this is not a joke, this is for real, I want you to come to a place where you will know your potential. I want you to know that there is something about you that needs to surrender to God, and you are going to see that wonderful working power of God after I am through with you. Yes you are a work in progress.

So Jesus puts Saul, yes that vicious Saul into a position of great discomfort, letting him feel the pain, letting him suffer, so that he can now pray, so that he can now look up! You're going through something right now? It won't kill you, in three days you're going to be all right, you're coming up out of it. Jesus sends the man of God to find him, look! Someone is coming in your direction, he is already halfway through his journey, in three days, watch out, that sickness, that problem, the tears, in three days, glory to God! Here the men brought Saul to the man and he performed a miraculous healing on Saul. God said, I will heal you Saul! I am able to heal you of your blindness, I am God! So the man of God, Ananias did what the Lord commanded him, he touched him and he was immediately healed. Saul not only received the wonderful gift of healing, he also received the blessed gift and power of the Holy Ghost, glory to God! From the experience he went through, he was now anointed by God.

Some may wonder why God would give a man such as Saul, his Spirit. Yet God can do whatever he wants to do. In fact, he changed Saul's name to Paul which means small, instead of being a man driven by power and political might,

God turned things around for his glory, reshaping his life, giving him a new beginning. God is still in the life changing business! The miraculous works of God changes the hearts of evil, men into men that are touching lives and fighting now for the cause of Christ.

When you receive a powerful demonstration from God like that of the Apostle Paul, you have no desire other than to proclaim the great gospel of the love joy and peace that you've found. If, when you taste of Christ and you are not compelled to telling others about Him, you need to go back for another taste of Him. Paul had never hesitated spreading the word of the transforming power of God. He was anointed by God, preached at Damascus, the same place that Jesus appeared to him, he began to preach Christ. He was on a mission to fight for a wrong cause but God turned his mission upside down and oh, he had no trouble telling other's about this great experience.

Now something rather strange was happening, people that knew Paul, knew his reputation, his brutal pass, saw him preaching and were astonished. This could never be real, the man that was killing, hurting, inflicting pains on the people of God, stands to defend the same gospel! They were sore afraid to accept Paul's transformation. In fact, it took Paul quite a while for even Christians to believe that he was serious. "Well maybe this is to trick us, he just wanted to get us cornered, and he just wanted us to fall for his tactics so he can kill us. We won't go anywhere close to him because he's evil." Yet, God has a way of doing strange things; he will take an evil heart and change it to good, and use it for his glory.

Can nobody fight in the kingdom of God like those that were radical for the devil? Yes many will fight to a degree, yet once you get a touch of the Holy Ghost and you become a warrior, in the Anny of the Lord your fighting ability gets to a new level. Paul began a fighting exhibition, he never ceased to fight! So here the Jews are plotting to kill our new Christian brother Paul because they've lost one of their soldiers yet he never backed down, his mind and motive were centered on mission. You can never defeat the anointed of God, God will always make a way of escape, they came looking for Paul but God had it that he was let down by the wall in a basket. God will provide a basket for your escape. You can never interrupt the works of God! God protects his own.

After Paul's conversion, even though he had been to Jerusalem in his old sinful state, he went back in his changed state, and this was hard for many to understand what had happened to Paul. Could the transforming power of God works on Paul? Then certainly it must be good, because if Paul could be changed, then anyone else no matter how vile he might be, there is hope for him. Is there anything that is too hard for God? Could Paul reached too far in sin that the grace of God couldn't reach him? Oh! We know that where sin abound, grace is much more abound. Grace will come to find you wherever you are, and he will snatch you up and love on you and you'll never be the same. Grace is for murderers, it is for muggers, yes, grace is just available to you and to me. Grace is for Paul! Thank you Jesus! The man that God cleanses, you must believe it, it is for real.

There is no gaming with God my friends, he loves to transform lives. Here you've got this ex-radical in the midst, he will bring the fight to the devil. Anywhere on earth that he travels he was bold enough to talk and testify about the Lord Jesus Christ. Paul went on to Seleucia, he went to Cyprus, and he also went to Salamis. In his traveling he went to the Isles unto Paphos, preaching and healing and casting out demons. Paul traveled to Antioch of Pisidia preaching in the synagogue on the Sabbath day. Paul stayed busy, in fact he never rested, and he was a true and dedicated fighter. A man truly on a mission. Paul traveled to Iconium, went to Lystra and every corner of the world spreading the good news of the Master and Savior Jesus Christ.

When you are known as a true fighter you will face many obstructions. There will be traps waiting to impede your ability to execute "blows" to the enemy. Paul and his companion Silas were thrown into prison. A man destined to be great will even suffer imprisonment. When you are doing the things that will make a difference in God's Kingdom, standing up for God, preaching with conviction, healing the sick and exposing to people their sin, you are a target, you will be hated! The world hated Jesus and so as a follower of the Lord, you will also be hated, you will be persecuted. How does a true fighter react in times of great persecution? Paul and Silas even in the prison cell, they did not shut their mouths, O, they worshipped and lifted up praises to God.

Though they were in chains guarded by soldiers, still the power of the Almighty God was never bound. Walls or metal and even men armed with weapons will never be able to stop the very presence of the Holy Spirit, to move and stir in the strangest way. These men were praising God in the beauty of holiness. Oh the wonderful power of God, he is awesome, oh yes he is! The power of God came down, the

"Shekhinah" glory of God's manifested presence came down in midst of them, overflowing, an outpouring. You never experienced anything like that I guess, it was a Holy Ghost explosion! A mighty showing up of God's power.

It is true that when two men that are radical, not worrying about their surroundings, not thinking about their geographic location, only interested in, "where the Spirit of the Lord is, there is liberty." Liberty even in the cell, they just began praising God, opening their mouths, singing songs of praise, and offering to God the fruits of their lips, it is true saints, that God that dwells in the midst of the praise. There is something special about the sound of praise that is coming from your pains, a praise that comes from the belly, and a praise that comes from the deep. David said, out of the depths will I cry! Crying from the whales belly like Jonah. It reaches God and it's a wonderful smell to his nostrils. Please don't get all burdened down, all bogged down in your cares and situations, just begin to praise God, open your mouth and praise God. Something is about to happen! Paul and Silas, laden in stripes and bruises, never deterred those men from praising God. Anger and intimidation would have never stopped them. In fact they were not operating with their own strength, they were functioning under a supernatural anointing that could never be turned off or turned down. At midnight! Some of your greatest breakthrough will come at midnight.

Have you ever opened up with a midnight praise celebration to God? A midnight prayer, when the enemy thought that he got you in his web, you're on your knees praying! At midnight when you should be worrying about all the bills and the children, you are on your knees before God! God will see you then and he will come in and join in that party, Oh yes it's true. In moments like those the anointing of God will be contagious, as you praise, look and see how even your family and loved one's suddenly are compelled to join in. God inhabits the praises of his people! Suddenly, there was a great earthquake so that the foundations of the prison were shaken and immediately all the doors were opened and everyone's bands were loosed. Now that's raw Holy Ghost, my friends! God burst open the prison doors with the keys of praise, and yes, he'll do it again because he is God by himself! Just imagine the experience, the natural man just cannot understand the mighty acts of God's power, it's not a joke, it's for real! You can't hold in chains, the very anointed of God, when the man of God calls his attention in prayer he responds, he makes it known even in the acts of an earthquake! Oh, don't let us start the praising and the praying, if you're not ready for the move of God, the building will shake! Bonds will be loosed! Jailers, you better do what you have to do, it's almost midnight sirs, you need to remember that we have a custom to be praising and worshipping. If you stay around long enough, we're going to pray, watch out, you might just get caught in a mighty earth quake, make up your mind, Mr. Jailer!

This is the Paul that God saves to be a better fighter than before. He was a fighter, but once God got a hold on your life, you'll never be the same, you're fighting attitude will be different. Once God touches you with his finger of love, even your motivations are changed, you become radical for God, fighting now in his army. If you profess to be God's soldier and not fighting for God, you are not yet trained, you do not know what true fighting is all about. When you want to be acquainted with this ability to fight in the spirit ask the Apostle Paul for some Holy Ghost instructions. That man will tell you how to be a winner. Yes, you'll never lose another fight if you get in touch with the one that stills the water. Remember the Jesus that calms the angry sea, the one that speaks to the wind and it obeys his voice. This power comes from the Lord Jesus Christ.

Paul said, for the weapons of our warfare are not carnal but mighty through God to the pulling down of strongholds, casting down imagination and every high things that exalts themselves against the knowledge of God and bringing into captivity every thought to the obedience of Christ. If you're on the

Lord's side, then you're on the winning side. He never lost a battle. Stand still and see the salvation of the Lord your God. God will use even an earthquake in his battle plan to deliver his children and nothing the jailers can do will stop God's plan.

You may think that after that experience it would slow those mighty warriors down, true fighters, my friend, will never slow down, they were called by God, prepared and sent on a mission, a mission that doesn't stop because of a great faith test. When your faith is rooted into the sure foundation of the Lord Jesus, a faith test will be a great motivation for the men of God destined to fight in the army of the Lord. Paul and Silas, had never allowed tribulation to force them into losing sight of their vision to be real soldiers of God.

Having the Lord on your side, it is important to remember that the energy source is still flowing, Like Paul, he went about his missions with the ideal plan of winning souls. Paul Went to Thessalonica preaching the word of God, there he faced many oppositions, so he fled to Berea, still fighting for souls. A man on a mission will not stop the fight due to oppositions, he presses on! The fight never stops my friends. At no time can you quit, in the journey of your faith, opposition means motivation because the source of strength comes from God and quitting is not, or should not be an option. When the going gets tough, the tough get going, glory to God! If we develop an attitude like this brother Paul, his zest for fighting was so rooted in his past, he recognized that in sin he was a warrior, therefore in righteousness he must be a double warrior, because once he began to think of what the Lord had done for him, it compelled him to fight even greater.

When you understand that you should have died in your trespasses and sins and God rescued you out of the pit of hell, you can't help it, you become excited about winning souls. The Bible said, "He that winneth souls is wise!"[33] The opposition in Thessalonica could not stop Paul, so he went even further to places like Corinth, where he stayed for a year and a half. This tells me that the brother was enjoying what he was doing as a true Disciple of the Lord Jesus. Your Christian faith must be excited and enjoyable. Paul never stopped traveling, he went to Syria and to the countries of Galatia and Phrygia. Paul visited Ephesus preaching Christ, laying hands upon the people and they received the Holy Ghost. After his conversion, Paul stayed quite busy traveling from place to place, city to city, he went through riots, had been through attacks of many kinds, and yet his faith in God could not be shaken. It was rooted in what was revealed through the power of the Holy Ghost. The Apostle Paul was thrown out of the temple in Asia, beaten bloody to the point of death, he was bound with chains, humiliated, yet was still fighting.

Yes, it is a fact that your brother Paul knew all the elements and factors of what a true and genuine fighter is all about. You are to know the true essence of suffering my

---

[33] Proverbs 11.30

friend, like Paul, through it all his faith in God remained firm, and his faith in God was relentless! While he was standing before the Roman Court, Paul defended himself though they cried out for his death, through the power of God he prevailed, though smitten by them. Many plots were made against Paul to take his life, he did escape by the divine providence of the Almighty God, he was sent to the Governor in Rome where he was imprisoned in Herod's Judgment Hall. That too could not have shaken his faith, still he remained faithful and was completely committed to the service of the Lord. Absolutely nothing this man faced could have deterred him from pursuing his ministry to God. He could not be stopped or slowed down by things he suffered. Paul was completely sold out to be that mighty warrior to the God he serves.

Protecting Your Vitality

Chapter Seventeen

As I've lived my life so far, I am saddened due to the constant shifting not only in the condition of society's moral standing but to the extent of which great men are destroying themselves. The very fabric of our society is fast decaying as men are losing their reputation, abandoning the very foundation and principle that have molded them throughout their life only by exposing their most sacred and treasured secrets. Our great ancestors often uses these sayings, "never let your right hand know what your left hand knows." Such sayings seem humorous or quite ambiguous at times, yet they speak boldly to the consciousness and awareness of our people; speaking especially to the men who will assume leadership at some given time. Your vitality is given to you by God and is incumbent upon each one to shield himself from every threat regardless of how simple or evasive they might be.

When we understand with certainty our connection and the vine from which we sprang, it is important noting that we have a divine nature. This beloved, is our power source, like a "well, or spring," the true fountain of our souls. It flows in us life and this life if treasured my friends, must be safe guarded with the seal of the Power of the Holy Ghost and God should be the only partner in possession of our combination to unlock. Beloved, you are the temple of God and you are to keep it holy.

How dare you allowing the enemies to invade the natural spring which supply your anointing? Such a commodity is too costly to be left unprotected. Are you not aware that the enemy is working around the clock seeking for any available path that he can penetrate and clog your system? We must have our "BEWARE SIGN" posted on every corner of our fountains, making sure that the spies of the enemy cannot penetrate your territory because of it will somehow create pollution which will ultimately block the passage way to your blessing.

When there is a clogging in your line, an infested line with debris and foreign matters of all kinds, you'll find that you lose power and the Holy Spirit in you cannot operate effectively, your ability to discern is shot, in fact, in events that you must use the wisdom of God, you are likely to step out in your own way and further messed things up. A fountain cannot send forth bitter and sweet water at the same time. You cannot put new wine into an old wine skins. Our vessels are to be made clean for truly if we are to live in victory the temple of the Holy Ghost must be free of viruses. For us to move into the next level with God, we must be determined to live that consecrated life exhibiting a heart that keeps and maintains the highest standard of holiness so that the power in us can operate in full force. The Bible says out of your belly shall flow rivers of living water. Living water can only flow where the stream of that flow is holy.

We can never invite visitors in our circle who are desirous of our anointing but is unwilling to pay the price.

Only you can declare to the world what is the cost of your anointing. This just doesn't come cheap, there is a huge price, a huge sacrifice and self-denial. You have invested many sleepless nights laboring, weeping, to obtain this and many do not think they are ready or can manage to pay. We must make the right assessment of those we allow in our space so that power will not drain from us, but power will in fact be added to our power.

It is important that we recognize that which is buried in our spirit, the precious gift from God, and only those that are walking under the umbrella, and have been directed by the "pillar of fire and pillar of cloud" should be offered sanctuary. There is no room for error in this Christian journey, one mistake can be detrimental, and that's why a man destined for greatness must "prove all things." I have seen in the faith of Jesus where many just come to Christ having a hidden agenda, looking for something other than Jesus and their motives must be carefully screened and every fine prints be prayerfully analyzed. The enemy has strange weapons which he'll use on us that will corrode our anointing. These can be the most unusual, unexpected and underrated stuff that one would laugh and even frown at the thought that such a minor piece of object would create a spiritual havoc. We look for the big stuff when the enemy is coming at us with small undetected objects! The enemy brought Goliath, an empty giant!

Look at a man such as Samson with such a promised future, but was side-tracked to the point of oblivion. One cannot easily become so complacent holding themselves to the degree, "it won't happen to me." Even strong men are slain by her! Relaxation and ease will only create a safe haven for the devil to reside. If we should look on the miraculous conception and birth of the son Samson, we can see clearly that his mother was a barren woman at first and would earnestly seek God's intervention in this matter.

One can never imagine the awe, the refreshing relief and tranquil, that one such as her received news that she was with child. Immediately the emptiness was replaced with joy and glee. It is true in those day's that a wife will live in a state of anguish if she cannot satisfied her wifely obligation giving her husband a child, especially the blessing of a son. In most cases, it can be devastating and most likely her wounds could cut deep into her soul forever as she struggles with the desire to be the wife of her dream.

We remember Hanna Samuel's mother, how she painfully suffered before having the experience of bringing a son into the world. It was true she too was bitter, and most of all suffered from a deep rooted inferiority complex and low self-esteem. This overwhelming scenario concerning Manoah and his wife, Almighty God was in complete control of this timely impregnation. From time to time we've seen how through the power of God even barren women are given Children so that the purpose of God's plan can be made perfect. We may even look into the situation involving Rebekah, Isaac's wife, how she too among many others were barren, yet, God who is the giver of all good things, blesses them in the time he chooses for his glory.

Samson the man whom God blessed with super human strength after his birth. This same child was selected before birth as the one who would begin to deliver Israel from the Philistines. An angel of the Lord instructed his parents, "Behold, thou shalt conceive, and bear a son; and now drink no wine nor strong drink, neither eat any unclean thing: for the child shall be a Nazarite to God."[34] The Bible spoke of Samson having the spirit of God on him that when he was attacked by a lion, how he crushed the lion like it was a kid.

Samson killed a thousand Philistines with the jaw bone of an ass, he asked God for water when he got thirsty and God gave him water in the same jaw he used as his weapon. This man Samson, exudes significant strength that he could conquer nations and cities, yet, with all this anointing from God, Samson, like many other men was dealing with a deep rooted issue. It is true that a man though big and strong in stature, yet his heart and his emotion can tear him to pieces.

Strong men can become weak in certain areas. Samson went to Gaza a city of Palestine, a place where he knew he had a lot of enemies. How dangerous it is visiting places where the people there are out to kill you. Samson was very busy chasing down a harlot in an attempt to fulfill his sexual urges. You know that a harlot will force great men into streets they have no business going. You know you don't belong there, yet, for the love of a harlot, you'll go out your way, risking your life in a "danger zone." The man Samson, he went to sleep with a harlot in the enemy's camp. Yes, the anointed man that he was, filled with God's power! It happened, oh yes, it does happen!

We know of great men that's been found all over the world sleeping with prostitutes, (you, I am sure know of someone that's been a great mentor to you and to others who have a serious sexual problem and slept with a harlot before.) The enemy heard through the grapevine that Samson was in their city, what a wonderful opportunity to take advantage of

---

[34] Judges 13:7

this great catch. They called up all their men and sealed off the entire city so that Samson could never escape. See what happened when not only that you're married, but you're a child of God and chasing after some harlot? Yes, you're like the walking dead! Again, "On the count of a whorish woman, a man is brought to a piece of bread." Yet, even in the sinful nature of this poor man Samson, God's power was still with him. There, the enemy waited at every gate and corner of the city to assassinate the anointing of God, but, at midnight

Samson arose and with his super human strength, took down the doors and the gates of the city, he took the two post and all the bars, putting them on his shoulder, then took them to the top of the hill. Samson was, yes, undeniable, a bad man for real! This man never have fear of nothing. He definitely possess that "I don't care attitude." Have you ever found someone that just don't care? I am going no matter what you said!

Why do great men fall into the web of "harlotry?" As a man of God drifting towards the appeasement of the flesh, there's a harlot that's waiting who is assigned to captivate and to steal his focus away from his divine destiny. Remember that your destiny is under attack and that harlot will do strange and enticing things to a man that opens the door to her whoredom. Those things are wonderful to the flesh, the taste buds are like drugs, and they are very addictive to the emotional impulses. What they do, not only messes with your minds, they get to the core of your soul and it contaminates the soul to the extent that you cannot function in the anointing that is on your life.

A harlot will get you to a place where you're in a drought, in a "Spiritual recession." You have no more value, no more resources to fall back on and this leads to the man of God losing his power. The word of God warns us, touch not, handle not and taste not. If we could actually analyze the effects of a touch, how dangerous it is, we would do all we can never to touch what's not ours? A touch is deadly, one touch will lead you to another because a harlot's touch is different from every other touch. She'll touch you just one time and the effects of that one touch stays in your mind, stays in your spirit and will never go away, as you think about that one touch, you'll contemplate over and over then finally, like current, it's effects keeps pulling you away till you fall into the temptation again.

When the woman with the issue of blood touched Jesus, virtue left him, he said, some body touched me, because I feel virtue left my body!" In you, there's virtue and a harlot is possessed with a destructive force that will drain you of your substance and vitality. Something very special is taken from you once touched by a harlot. That's the reason why so many wonderful men are dead spiritually they are no longer themselves.

When you taste anything that concerns a harlot, you are indeed marked for life. The things that harlots carry brings with it a poisonous substance that as it reaches your spirit, your strength and power is at great risk. You are to protect your vitality, it is so essential. After any taste of her, you withdrew from her, thing that annoys your spirit. Then you began to experience that, instead of you focusing on your duties, you are now directing all your attention on her, you realized that your spirit is slow poisoned, that's why many around you are no longer on fire, the power went dead.

Next, you handle a harlot my friend, fire is involved, and it's a fire which wounds, cripples and even kills. This one is so severe since it leaves you in a confused state, bewildered and lost. Handling a harlot is truly the road that leads you to hell. You are so damaged that, neither the hospital nor any other institution can effectively spare you but for the cross of Calvary. If one finds himself on the road to "harlotry," it's never too late for him to return to the road that leads to Calvary.

The road to Calvary is accessible to all and those that was marred by the oppression and strong hold of sin can find the true path again. It's very funny that one touch of the harlot can destroy you for the rest of your life, yet just one touch of Christ can rescue the deepest sinner for the rest of his life and in fact for the rest of eternity. A man that stays drinking, consumed in the habit of drinking, whenever you see him he's drunk and staggering, overtime that liquor stays in his system and his body is immune to this substance, it may take some time and efforts to get his system back on the right tract. Not so with God, have we not remembered the woman with the issue of blood, she was suffering for so long, spending all her livelihood on doctors and medicines. She heard about Jesus and desires to get close to him for a miracle, she pressed her way in the large crowd and all she could grab hold on was the hem of his garment, and that quick, she did not need to have a follow up, therapy, other counseling or any other assistance, that one touch was all she needed to change the course of her life forever. One touch is good but it depends on who you're touching or who's touching you! The master Jesus touch you, you are no longer the same. Something happened and oh, I know, Jesus touched me and made me whole.

A touch from God will automatically put you back in line, put you on the road to success, put you on the road to be productive again, shattered dreams and visions will all spring forth again. Very unfortunate, so many are wounded, while handling the harlot, their hopes have been faded, they've lost their power to be great, then finally they wind up having a dead spirit, no life in their words, the very substance of their souls becomes dry. There is an unwanted touch that will get into your spirit and will create anguish and misery that is irreparable.

Please, don't ever get too close to a harlot unless for the purpose of evangelism, anything else, you'll be enticed by her stuff. Her lips, her perfume, her very attire, she's always exposing herself in ways to trap the man of God, watch out for those exposures, they're deadly. Not only that, but there's something about their hands, they got some kind of evil magic in them, that they'll use and as the magic works to their benefit, you get overly relaxed, become drowsy and start to sleep.

My God, when you fall asleep in a harlot's lap, you're in danger, yes, you're in serious trouble. That's the worst thing that can happen to you, as you sleep, you smell, you inhale, you are smeared, and as you sleep she now gets the opportunity to dope you with the poison of hell! Why do you see countless men, your sons, your husband, your father, acting very strangely? You wonder in dismay, that's not the man I grew to love. Is he just getting old or lost interest in the family? No, they have been to the enemy's camp and have fallen into "harlotry!" He's no longer the kind and happy man that he used to be, there's a problem of great proportion and he must be helped and that's right now! You won't lose that son, you won't lose that husband or that father, all he needs is a real touch from one that is sent with healing in his hands, one that speaks to the heart of the problem, who speaks peace that will restore, enlightens and set free.

What was your brother Samson doing with that harlot? Samson, that fine young man, handsome. His parents loved that boy so much, (you know how our parents are with us boys?) They want the very best for him and would do anything for him to get it. He got real wonderful locks that today, girls just love nice looking locks, especially when it's properly groomed. This son could have any of the finest sisters around, but, some boys just can't hear and some just can't be satisfied. Samson left his own circle, the nice sisters that he was raised with, chasing after the enemies daughter. You know they don't like you, they're out to get you, what are you doing in their town? We must be careful where we're going to pursue a wife! A man that is destined for greatness, must choose carefully what territory, what tribe his wife will come from. Abraham warned his son Isaac not to get his wife from the Canaanites, Isaac told his son Jacob also not to choose a wife from the Canaanites. It does make a significant difference, those that we attach ourselves to, and our fathers know that quite well. Samson was told of that danger as well.

Have you ever had a rebellious son or daughter? Rebellion is the sin of witchcraft, it's a terrible sin my friend! Samson was rebellious, this man wouldn't listen to his parent. How often do we see this kind of attitude displayed in our very eyes? You can talk to that son, that daughter till Jesus comes, they won't take heed. Son, don't be stupid, you can't take a wife from the enemy's camp, I'm telling you, don't do it son! Daddy even gets mad, Mother keep praying and as they struggle together to convince their children, that they love them so much and just want to help because they foresee the danger, you still let your parents down. Samson, is there no daughter among your people for you to choose'? Samson, would you just stop being so stubborn? You are very handsome Samson, all the girls in the community want to check you out, are you saying that none of these fine sisters deserves your attention? You've gone to school together, they understood your culture, they got your interest and they'll do anything to make sure you're successful. With all that information, Samson still strayed into the enemy's camp, lusting after the Philistines' daughter. Here my friend, the Philistines had a very serious conflict with the Children of Israel. As a young man, you do not understand the culture of their people and they are dangerously out to destroy you.

Remember the Lord spoke to us in regards to strange women and how we are to deal with wisdom. Strange women do strange things, but when your mind is fixed on doing something you love, nothing seems to penetrate your heart to stop you. Why do men want what they want, do what they want, when they want? Many times we know that we are wrong, yet, we defend our wrong anyway, yielding to the temptations and suffer the terrible consequences that we could have avoided.

Many times even Christians use the Holy Spirit as an excuse; "the Holy Spirit spoke to me," and we even lied on the Holy Ghost! It's true, we do! Let's be for real here, in the context of Samson, as the word reflects, mixed marriages by Israelites with other races were forbidden, and as men, we're not trying to hear that from our parents, even when we know they are right. We go on arguing, saying, "Mom you're right, but this is me, let me deal with it, I am grown, so we thought? Mom still tries to reason with the boy, "You tell me you must go and take a heathen woman from the Philistine people who constantly oppressed Israel? Are you willing to join with the oppressors, will you be willing to pay the price?" Are you really serious Samson? Well, we can argue it was to accomplish God's will, let's see, the Bible says, "Whoso findeth a wife findeth a good thing, and obtaineth favour of the Lord"[35] Yes, but, does this always means findeth a wife of the daughter of the enemy? Is there no daughter among your people Samson?

Strange women are after your vitality Samson! They're going to get you son! They are interested in knowing your protected secrets, where your strength lies? It seems so crazy, but the truth is, so often men make the awful mistake starting out their lives having wonderful friendships with many daughters of their own cultures and background. These daughters supported them, defended them while they were also a great comfort to them through their struggles. They have always been with them in their time of darkest despair. These daughters understood their pains and hurts, they sympathized with their frustrations and in most cases sacrificed themselves for the good of their promotion. Yet, as they arrived to the top, achieving various success, they run into the arms of the Philistines daughter, they forget so quickly who was there when they were looked down at, they forget who was there when life was a burden.

Very sad but true, when you become "twisted" broken down like that old truck, that needs to be junk, when you're wounded by the strange Philistine woman, you try sneaking back into the clutches of the same wonderful daughter that you've rejected.

You know that your loving sister is always compassionate and in tenderness they'll show mercy, it's their nature, but why break their wonderful hearts big brother Samson? Give that sister that nurtures you a chance, come on Samson, feel her heart! Many times you know that you are wrong, you know she's the only person that has your

---

[35] Proverbs 18.22

interest at heart, yet the temptation of that strange woman that you allow lust and pride to fill your heart forcing you into giving up your secrets.

You've always been strong and successful with your sister because she gave you the energy you needed, what that strange woman did is drained you of your vitality. Yes you remember, you have always been productive until you went to the enemy's camp, now nothing good seems to be happening for you son, what's wrong? The stone that the builders rejected, will become the chief corner stone. Remember your sister my friend, she's your corner stone, she will stand by you even when you've violated. Sisters looked at you through the eyes of mercy, she saw you in the eyes of grace.

Though you might be wounded right now due to the mistakes you've made, Samson, what will you do when your sister rebuilds you again? Can you in humility acknowledge your faults? Submit and live! Now with the right understanding and grateful attitude, move on and live Samson.

So, what happens here? The Philistine's daughter, she loves you to death, I know you thought she does, well, just when the heat turns up, see what side or whose side is she on. She must choose to live, she and her family or will she defend you no matter what? Well, buddy, you're on your own, she tells you straight up that her family comes first. I must be loyal to my people, you think you're my husband and all, but, in this case someone must take the heat and that's not me and my family, that's what she said. Home girl sold poor Samson out! Have you ever been sold out before? That's tough! When that happens you becomes angry, what? I can't believe she did this! What, you can't believe she did this, what did you think in the first place, she's not as dedicated as you thought? They're in it for the money, and the opportunity. The next chance she gets, you will be history son.

We always get caught out there by their beauty, we are weak to unknown fake beauties, when she begin to cry, we get weak by her tears, we melt as she begins to cry, not knowing that it's her way of softening us so she can feed you to the dogs. Seductions! "Tell me your secrets, they won't know." Lie! She persistently persuaded him and he suddenly fell for the lies. The strongest man in history melted at her seducing approach. That's the truth, they know how to get you, they know the right words to say and the right things to do pulling your secret out from you. She don't need to torture you, all she does is giving you the loving that you're chasing, weep as if she's in love, whine and Whine until poor Samson gave up his stuff. You can't give up your stuff, it's what sustains you, it's where the fountain of your anointing resides, protect your vitality, you will last much longer!! Solomon said, "For a whore is a deep ditch; and a strange woman is a narrow pit."[36]

---

[36] Proverbs 23.27

Employing a Winner's Attitude

Chapter Eighteen

In order to be a winner, one must operate through the eyes of the spirit. The man of God must continue to develop a winner's attitude in order to remain a true fighter. Being knocked down in the hard tracks of our lives we never always get knocked out. Even in the sad cases where we might have been knocked out unconsciously, knocked out cold, there is still hope if we will get back up and fight again. You might be down but not out?! As we looked at the wonderful expressions of the Apostle Paul, we realize the many times he was seriously knocked down, yet we saw by his knocking down, that he had constantly risen up with a greater zeal and agility to stay in the ring and fight. We come to terms with the God given wisdom, that to be knocked down, can be where and how the power and anointing of God is to be supplied into the lifeless vessel. That might be where you'll be filled up with an outpouring that can be lasting, good and effective.

Paul the Apostle understood what was at stake had he stayed down in the ring and refused the call of the Lord

Jesus. When he asked him, "What will thou have me to do?" That my friend was very real and serious coming from Paul. When you're at the place of surrender, all you can think about is what you can do to remedy the situation. This experience was certainly for a good cause, as Paul declared that he heard the sound of a voice speaking and it was not just an ordinary voice. It seemed that although Paul was living his life conducive to the flesh, he recognizes it was truly the voice of the Living God.

It is very vital that we get this clear, when the Lord speaks, something significant happens. Jesus often speaks to his people under strange circumstances, and as he speaks, the very substance, that very sound, oh yes, his very breath is an indication that we are to get ready, because something is about to happen, that might be the beginning of greatness. One must be prepared to lose something in order to receive something from God. You must be ready to be emptied out in order that you can then be filled.

There lies in all of us some old selfish attitudes, self-wills, that old self-motivation and evil intentions which must be crucified so that an importation of God's will can be erected and manifested in us. We must then be so prepared to die, even in the act of a personal knock down, falling flat on our faces and thus alone can we be molded, becoming fit for the Lord to use us. Understandably so, if Christ will put a sinner on the cutting table, put him on the wheel or even on the road to Damascus, well my friend, fear not, because God is staying right there with you. You will never have to go through that dark tunnel all by yourself, God will do all the necessary directing, so that you'll come out as fine gold. Yes, he will see you through those afflictions and the fruit yields in your tomorrow will be much better than before. The plans of God are to bless you beyond measure.

God is never attached to the business of hurting you, he will chasten those that he love, he will cause you to go through some fire and certainly some storms, but as you go through them, you are assured that they won't kill you, they will only make you better. No chastening for the present is enjoyable, daddy means you well, he will have to do some spanking but that doesn't mean that dad loves you any less. Love will sometimes make dad have to get a little tough, and after all the little pains , your life will indeed be a mirror for others to look through, live and be productive.

You need to accept and rejoice over your Damascus experience, it is for your good! The shocking truth is that some pains in life are necessary, they are to mold and shape us into God's perfect image, and we must seek going through them with the least amount of sorrow, the joy of a true fighter! Even though you might be aware of its painful nature, yet the anticipated blessing compels you to rejoice, and praising God who is leading you into victory. You are to have that attitude, leaping and glorifying the King of Kings, knowing that there's a blessing in the storm.

To a great extent, I believe that Paul's life could have been ended when considering his past non caring attitude. His sinful motives could have cost him a great deal while he continued his act of opposing and oppressing the people of God. This man was riding his horse in a callous attempt at creating havoc on God's people. Having that encounter with the Lord at such a time, in a state of provocation could have been detrimental. Still the plans of God are always to save even the chief of sinners. Christ hands are stretched out still and those that will come to him he will never turn aside. I thought somebody once said, there is room at the cross for me, though millions have come there's still room for more.

We remember the famous Apostle Paul, called himself a wretched man.

There's room for all in Jesus, glory to God! We'll find mercy and grace at the feet of Jesus, that's why you can never go too far in sin that grace is unable to reach you. The Bible said, "Where sin abounded, grace did much more abound!"[37] It's highly unlikely, impossible that you will ever completely exhaust the stock pile of grace as a sinner. Mercy will still reach down in the gutters and grab a desperate sinner and put his shattered life back to together, those broken pieces, oh yes, mercy will mend and you'll never be the same in the eyes of mercy. The nature of God is to rescue, even if you've violated the people of God, he will still show mercy, he hears the heart's cry, acquainted with the tears you shed. The touch that Paul received from God, causes him to get up and begin to walk into the great calling, he realizes that in this great walk he doesn't need to destroy lives, he now joins the rescue mission!

What's better than to be able to touch souls and lay hands on them in the Name of the Lord Jesus? It is important that a person coming to Christ, that he count the cost. Paul counted the cost and he realizes that the cost of following Christ was huge. There are many trials and great testing to suffer and once you endure them, the Lord said you will be blessed, that's why Paul gladly accepts his call to salvation.

What a privilege to turn from sin and just humbly follow in the leading of our Lord, it take a bold step of faith! Paul was beaten, stoned, threatened, and imprisoned. Slapped in the face, stripped of his dignity, destitute, thrown out of the synagogues. Yet the heart that a fighter in the Holy

---

[37] Romans 5.20

Ghost possessed, can never be uprooted under excruciating circumstances. The fighter in whom Paul was made causes him to express love and compassion even to his accusers. He was able to preach the good news of salvation to King Agrippa, that's the transforming power of God!

While the Apostle Paul was sailing on the stormy sea, he knew not only how to deal with the boisterous winds and tempest of life, he also possessed the right attitude when the wind became contrary in the open sea. On the raging sea, one must remember you have the Lord Jesus on the ship. He is right there with you, and you will not fall, you will not drown. Can you remain firm like Paul in that situation? You must be confident that greater is he that is in you than he that is in the world!

When you face tough situations, you are to stand strong and encourage those around not to be fearful! Paul comforts his companions on that boat, be ye of good cheer, there shall be no loss of any man's life among you! That's a man that is bold and brave, an act of confidence! In the midst of the storm the man that has an encounter with God new that it will be peace, yes it will be peace in the storm, I shall not be greatly removed! In the storms of life my friends, even when the winds are altogether farce, just like the Lord had spoken to that wind, he still has the power to speak today, you just cannot second guess whether the Lord will speak or not, we've seen and heard Him, His voice is still real gentle, especially when we are hurting. Immediately the sea stood still at his direct command. Jesus said, in me, you may have peace, in the world you will have trials, but be of good cheer, I have overcome the world.[38] We can never (no matter how hard we might try), escape the hard trials of this life, yet the

---

[38] John 6: 33

man of God owning that Godly assurance, can be assured and walks in that confidence no matter the darkness and gloom, we knows the master is there to take you through. Sometimes it's very strange that as you've won a victory, there goes the enemy coming back at you over here with yet something even greater. Yes you've just gotten over, and you think that life will now be better, here the attack comes right back at you. This is very confusing and it will create discouragement, yet Paul faces that same dilemma, trouble on every side. Paul, I will cause a great ship wreck. Paul will you allow a ship wreck to uproot your faith in God?

Will the shipwreck of your life uproot and destroy your faith in the God that you serve? I thought you were serious when you said, "All things works together for good!" I thought you said, "I can do all things." Well even in these moments, I can guarantee you that the power of God will unfold before your very eyes and the shipwreck can be just what the Lord prescribes for your healing.

Sometimes you must be broken for you to be made whole, yes you must sometimes be wounded, in order to be strengthened! O what are you talking about? How is this possible? A plant must die to produce fruits. Jesus must die to give eternal life, the way to prosperity is struggle! A man can say in his heart, I am purposed to fight and be joyful about it. However, as the times of his test increases, you might think that this one is not just a storm, this seems like a hurricane, " a number seven magnitude like hurricane," the velocity of the wind is ferocious knocking down everything you've spent all those years building, will you keep your word and be continuously dependable?

Struggle should never cause you to abandon your faith. You will be tested beyond measure, do remember that Paul immediately escaped the greatest shipwreck of his life and as he walked on land he was suddenly attacked and bitten by a dangerous viper. You might say it was better that he stayed on sea a bit longer, but as long as it would have taken him, that viper would be waiting on him. It seems like no other person will suffer for you, what was meant to be your trial. The man was just rejoicing. I can imagine him praising God for bringing him through that one yet, Satan was right there waiting with the intention of bringing upon him yet another hard trial. Let me tell you something, there is a cross that we all have to carry and sometimes believe me, it can be heavy! There's Misfortune after misfortune, will you remain faithful my friend at that time, something is about to happen, for weeping may endure for a night but joy comes in the morning! You need to see your trials as the right thing for your triumph and step over them as though you already won the victory. What did somebody say? "Trials only come to make you stronger!"

As you fight in the Christian journey, know with all certainty that even if bitten by venomous beasts, the God of heaven never cease from caring, he's setting you up for greatness! Like Paul, you must shake it off, you will not die, neither you will not be defeated because the Lord is on your side.

Paul was known to be the greatest fighter, owning to himself a passion and conviction that everything in this life belongs to God. He said, "I am crucified with Christ, nevertheless, I live, yet not I, but Christ liveth in me and the life which I now live in the flesh, I live by the faith of the son of God who loved me and gave himself for me."[39]

---

[39] Galatians 2.20

Paul's attitude as a true fighter was never a "himself" focus. He said that he died with Christ! His life was hidden with Christ in God! This brother new what suffering was all about though, he have seen and enjoyed a firsthand life of luxury, he understood in retrospect that the best life that one can live in the flesh is one lived for God. The greatest joy, the greatest pleasure for Paul as he said, "that I may know him!" Paul wants to get to the place to know Christ in totality; his hunger and deepest yearning was to get to that place, striving to know him. Regardless of his present condition, he would never retire into self-pity and reservations, I just want to know the deep things of the Lord and that was his real aim; I just want to tap into the power of his suffering and his resurrection! Glory to Jesus!

The mentality of a true fighter must be that of confidence. You know who the enemy is and that he's using his natural, selfish ability to oppress the people of God. In Paul's case, he was secure in the fact that Satan couldn't just penetrate his life doing just about anything to this great fighter. He made that bold statement, "I am more than a conqueror!" With this kind of attitude, Paul recognized it would take him through whatever situation he may encounter. It doesn't mean that all the trials that come your way you automatically will win them, yet a conqueror's heart will allow you to stand in the face of evil and look into the face of the enemy and say, Yea though I walk through the valley of the shadow of death, I will fear no evil!" Knowing that God has not given you the spirit of fear, but of love, power and sound mind. You can confront the enemy with certainty, it's the fact that you know the Lord is fighting alongside you every step of the way.

Are you that one that is more than a conqueror only when things are only going fine? It's easy to be that way then, but until you are tested and are still standing, then you demonstrates to the world, a conqueror's heart because you won't back down in difficult times, no you won't quit, but every time the enemy takes a punch, you are punching back and even if you can't punch back, you just jab and cover your face. You refuse to stay down because that's what the old dragon wants, and you just cannot give him his desire. Get up and fight even harder! The Apostle Paul had endured

some of the most crucial and daunting circumstances that life could offer, it was at the very lowest place in his faith walk that he made a Victor's triumph, "I am more than a conqueror," such an utterance rings loudly from the deepest part of his spirit. Even when you're knocked down, when you're at your wits end, you can still maintains that conquerors attitude and been motivated to face the next challenge. Yes it's true, in some of the most horrifying circumstances that the enemy throws at Paul, with prayer and faith, he stood there and analyzed his strategies, he waited in anticipation, not trying to do anything in a hurry but surrendering was never part of his plans. As the dark clouds came crashing down on the servant of God, Paul looked up and called them, "these light afflictions!" Yes, these light afflictions, that's what the man calls problems on every side! The brother had been stoned, imprisoned, beaten, suffered shipwreck, thorns in the flesh, bitten by vipers, had a slew of atrocities inflicted upon him, yet to him they are "light!" oh yes, you talk about a man with strong resolve, determination and strong will, that was the Apostle Paul.

    You may never experience in your life time, a storm or a deep trial that can be compared to anything that Paul faces, yet we sometimes crumble into isolation at the slightest issue that comes our way. The minor infractions are only to test and to provoke in your spirit, a greater zeal that will accomplish greatness for the kingdom of God. The way we respond to our struggles speaks volume, in fact it also demonstrates our relationship with God. Paul uses the analogy of light afflictions. "For our light affliction, which is but for a moment, worketh for us a far more exceeding and eternal weight of glory."[40] Paul went on further and stated, while we look not at the things which are seen, but at the things which are not seen, for the things which are seen are temporal, but the things which are not seen is eternal.

That's a fighter's attitude! Eternal! Your attitude is heaven bound. Paul's attitude supersedes that of today's mentality whose focus is in the now. I must win every battle right now! I must have it now! I just don't want to pray today, I want to pray tomorrow and pray again until it happens. A fighter must show diligence and ferocity. Though our outward man perishes, yet the inward man is renewed day by day. To pattern Paul's example and to wrestle and contend with the enemy in the struggle towards victory, our hearts must be carefully set on Christ. That no matter how we see things with our natural eyes, we know that with Christ you are always on the winning side. You just can't loose with Jesus Christ on your team, my friend, that's just totally impossible, you are undefeated! When we stop to think of the Apostle Paul's courageous attitude, there is multitudes of evidence relating to his fighting attitude. He took his afflictions in such a joyous mode, for this he said: "But what things were gain to me, those I counted loss for Christ . . . I count all things but loss for the excellency of the knowledge of Christ Jesus my Lord, for whom I have suffered the loss

---

[40] 2 Corinthians 4:17

of all things and do count them but dung, that I may win Christ."[41]

How often we never win because we take the wrong approach? We know that if we stay on course, we are bound to win, yet many times allowing distractions and our many cares and insurmountable burdens causing us to get off course. As long as you are certain of the team that you are on, you can't afford to drift off course, you just can't afford to let down and hurt our team, especially those that loves us the most. We are to abide by that same principle that governs the good of the team. We're to, at all times pull in the same direction. Paul said: "I count not myself to have apprehended: but this one thing I do, forgetting those things which are behind, and reaching forth unto those things that are before, I press towards the mark for the prize of the high calling of God in Christ Jesus."[42] That's a winner's attitude, you can't afford to be holding on to the things of the past. Those hurts and pains of the past will only stop the growth of the future. If we are willing to let go, we are thus preparing ourselves and sustaining our energies to become more driven for an excellent future.

When we empty ourselves then God will pour into us his promised greatness. We must also strive like Paul, to develop steadfastly the winner's attitude of contentment. We can't worry about everything, every setback, every opposition, every hurt and at the same time be a winner. Contentment will feed your spirit man, and ultimately you'll be better able to deal with life's challenges. Paul went on to tell us that he himself has developed the skill to be content in whatever state he found himself. The man testified that he

---

[41] Philippians 3.7
[42] Philippians 3.13-14

can do all things through Christ that strengthens him. How can one second guessed or even have the nerve to implied that these principles Paul employed would somehow cause you to loose in the fight'? God is giving you the strength and the agility to fight, and with his power, you can never fail. God is the one that supplies us with an abundance of strength.

I love it when Paul said it best, "But my God shall supply all your needs according to his riches in glory by Christ Jesus." With a heart of contentment, you must win my friend! Having a heart of gratitude, just being simple and roll with life's storms, God will speak peace and you'll find courage and motivation to go on.

As we ponder upon the life and legacy of the Apostle Paul, we realize the strength and determination which he maintains, living the life that would please the Lord at all times Never mind the many challenges that life would sometimes bring, he stayed in the fight, never giving up. We should seek on a constant basis to be looking pass our many afflictions understanding that they are necessary to accomplish God's purpose.

A story was told about a donkey that was born, the creature heard a voice say, "I have something great for you to do." As he grew older, he kept wondering what it was and he kept asking God about it. The donkey was curious as to finding out what was this great plan. This occurred three times until finally the donkey died. Then one day a man named Samson reached down and picked up the jaw bone of the donkey, using it to slew thousands of his enemies. We were also told of three large trees that had great plans for the future to be great. One wanted to be a treasure chest to holding great treasure. One wanted to be a ship that carried kings across oceans. Finally, the next wanted to stand on top of a mountain so everyone could see how great he was. When the woodsmen came and cut down the first tree, he began to rejoice for he was going to be made into a treasure chest, until he realized that they weren't making him into a treasure chest. Instead they made him into a manger. Likewise, the second tree was cut down also and was disappointed in learning that it would not be used for a ship, instead it would be used for a boat. Finally the third, they just cut off a part of the tree and took it away. The first tree didn't become the treasure chest that he wanted to be, instead he held the greatest treasure of all time when they placed the baby Jesus inside the manger. The second tree didn't become the ship that he wanted to carry King's across the ocean, instead, he carried the King of King's, when Jesus sat inside that boat. Then the third tree didn't get to stand on top of a mountain for people to see his greatness, instead, Christ carried him and he stood on top of a hill called Golgotha so that scripture could be fulfilled. And so, he was on top of a hill for all to see the savior of the world, the wonderful son of the Almighty God. It is true that many times we reject our blessings because we look on the mountains of our circumstances and refuse to look on the big God that is bigger and more powerful than whatever it is that we face. A wonderful song written by Lynda Randle which really brought thrills my spirit, Life is easy when you're up on the mountain and you've got peace of mind like you've never known. But things change when you're down in the valley. Don't lose faith, for you're never alone. For the God on the mountain is still God in the valley.

When things go wrong, he'll make them right. And the God of the good times, is still God in the bad times. The God of the day, is still God in the night. We talk of faith way up on the mountain, talk comes so easy when life is at its best.

Now it's down in the valley of trials and temptations, that's where faith is really put to the test. Friends, the valley is where you need to stay prayed up! We are to remember that there are never and there will never be anything in life that the people of God can face that God will never give them the strength and courage to face. Paul was no different than us today yet, he was so very confident in the God he met on the road to Damascus. He revealed himself to him even in his sinful state as he caused oppression to his children. The transforming power of God redeemed him and many others from their destruction's. Paul could now live a sober life worthy to be called a son! How wonderful it is to know that God can take the vilest sinner and pour himself into them and in turn use them to accomplish greatness only for his glory.

It is not strange that Paul testified even in prison to: "Rejoice . . . and again, I say, Rejoice."[43] Considering how empty his life was without God, yet after finding out his goodness and the depths of God's love and how no matter where Paul found himself, he could turn to God in humility and demonstrate to the world a joy that only came to him through the power of God. A joy that no man can give, but can only be obtained by the divine power of Jesus Christ and his shed blood on the cross. This joy which motivates him to keep pressing on through life as more than a conqueror, Paul could boldly say at the end of his earthly journey, "I have fought a good fight!" He has, by the power of God triumphed over those obstacles, he overcame all odds, winning the victories over those oppressors, over those attacks. Paul was at a beautiful place in his life though he was old in age yet the life lived for Christ he concluded, there's no regrets. He

---

[43] Philippians 4.4

found out that he could only reigned with Jesus by taking up his cross, he withstood the test like a man. "I have fought a good fight, I have finished my course and I have kept the faith." a triumphant shout of victory, above everything else, Paul proclaims, "l have kept the faith!" Keeping the faith is the ultimate aim, when we see in life how very

easy it can be for one's faith to be uprooted. We can learn from Paul, that great test requires great faith, and a true fighter must understand that, when the going gets tough, the tough get going! When the going gets tough, it's not the time to quit. When the pressures of life become intensified, it's the time to muster up your spiritual muscles, roll up the sleeves and fight for your life. Your salvation is worth fighting for, your prosperity deserves fighting for, and you must believe that the resources in heaven are never depleted, heaven is never on a recession. But it takes radicalized attitude, an attitude taken by force, wrestling with or contending with the enemy, the "bear like mentality." When we develop our fighting maneuvers, we are to remember that Jesus, the Chief Commander of our lives compels us to pray and not faint, prayer is a worrier's greatest weapon, one that demolishes the forces of evil.

A fighter having all his equipment handy, prayer must be at the forefront for an accomplished victory. Paul said, we are wrestling not against flesh and blood but against principalities, powers and against the rulers of the darkness of this world against spiritual wickedness in high places. Paul understood the forces that you and I are up against, that's why we must prepare always for battle. He gave us the instructions which he knew is capable to get this job done, he taught us to put on the whole armor of God, and not to leave our tools or equipment for later, we must take the whole package, so that we may be able to withstand in the evil day. Well if you would asked me, we are certainly living in the "Evil days." As we speak and as we look around it is a day where men regard not the Lord.

As Disciples of Christ, we must be fully protected wearing the whole armor, so that the enemy will never penetrate our lives, blocking our potential and our drive towards spiritual success. Paul also said, we must stand! We must be firm, fully focused, do not fold and choke, giving any reason to the enemy, in fact, showing signs of vulnerability. Paul wants you to stand and be bold even in the face of despair, having your loins girt about with truth and having on the breastplate of righteousness. When we walk, we are to be cautious of our surroundings, having our feet protected, having the shield of faith and our helmet of salvation. You may never want to leave out the very valuable sword of the spirit which is the word of God. Mothers would always caution us that we are to take the words of God with us everywhere we go, and that is so true because it is the word that transforms our lives. Looking on the examples of the Apostle Paul, you can pattern your life from his to be a victorious fighter, he said, pray always! In his analogy, he uses wonderful military terms to illustrate his points because he understood that to be enlisted in the army you will likely have to fight. Yes, warfare is a must in the army of the Lord and training is very crucial if you want to win. The man new the dangers of fighting, he also knew the powers of fighting, and if when called to fight we are not ready, then we forfeit our blessings. We can never forget that a soldier must be ready to be deployed at any given moment, therefore preparation is of paramount importance as in any other army.

The Lord requires us to be in a state of readiness, so that as the Commander in Chief he will be well please with us having the right attitude representing him. God will be proud of his servants when we are bold, serving him in righteousness and truth, passion and conviction, marching on with victory sign, victory in out spirit, a divine shout of triumph on our lips and our hearts that swells up within us. I have fought a good fight, I have finished my course and I have kept the faith. Henceforth there is laid up for me a crown of righteousness, which the Lord, the righteous judge shall give me at that day. The fight is good! The fight is definitely a good one! Let's not be afraid to delve into the enemy's camp and take back what they have stolen. The kingdom of heaven suffers violent and the violent take it by force. Stay in the fight and never give in, you have a crown of righteousness that the Lord will give on that day and not for you only, but for all those that love his return. Give the Lord the praise and fight.

A Power Within Reach

℘

Chapter Nineteen

Scripture Reading: John 5.2-3, 5-9

It's very alarming that in this world, many are overly fascinated with the vast technological accomplishments of our time. Because of this progress, there are those who are slowly embracing scientific ideals in the offset, they are denying the very existence of the Almighty God. We are living in a computer age where at the flick of a button, messages can be transmitted from person to person. We can access information, making financial transactions and making purchases many times from the comfort of our homes due to the advance stages of technology. Technology in our world today is so advance that traveling to the moon, going into space is as simple and quick as if going on a trip to Mexico! It is true that man had developed such a system which pushes the world into discovering things that are mind-boggling. Ultimately, God is taken out of the equation, many caring not for the salvation of their souls, what is now a constant struggle to recognizing the power of the resurrection and the effects of the cross!

Certainly, there is no human technology that can somehow offer or supplement a precise path to eternal life except through the one that was provided for us by God Himself over two thousand years ago. The Eternal God that created the Universe, holds within His power the most accurate plan that will give man a destiny that will surpass this life to a place of eternal happiness. When God created this world and everything in it, it was something that neither government, politicians, scientist, nor any other technological sources could duplicate. It's not the *"Big Bang Theory."* It's not the *"Darwin Theory!"* It's an intelligent God who declares, "Let there be light and there was light!" Man may try to create some images gather a fabricated myth, or play on one's intellect, yet man will never find in a technological exploration any other means by which you can access eternal life but by the cross, by the blood, by the resurrection of Jesus Christ! Oh yes! They will never stop seeking because the resurrection of Christ is such an offense to their intelligence so whatever it takes "they'll poke some holes," yet, the power of God is and will be ever superior to every forces of this world!

Man had gotten so wise and advance in their views of the world yet, to their uniqueness cannot come to the place of understanding that a God so great as the King of Kings, are able to impregnate a virgin woman with the Holy Ghost, placing Himself into her womb and sending the Angel with a message to her espoused husband with the greatest news, "fear not Joseph to take unto thee Mary thy wife, for that which is conceived in her is of the Holy Ghost!" They will experiment with various kinds of scientific objects, conducting themselves in ways that are unseemly, unnatural and to the extent places limitations on the God that created the world.

Man would still reject the power of the resurrection claiming it is impossible, undermining the one with such power to speak the world into existence. There are however, those that still believe when Jesus said, "destroy this temple and in three days l will rebuild it!" He was for real! Yes, it is still one of the most striking, historical event that ever took place on earth, it strikes at the very core of the enemies of God, the *"Resurrection of Jesus Christ!"* Some two thousand years ago, Jesus died and was buried in a sealed tomb, but on the third day Jesus Christ burst that tomb with His power and He rose up triumphantly and there is nothing that technology of today can do about it because the grave could not hold Him, the power which raises Christ was like dynamite! His resurrection was that of a great explosion, dynamis[44] power! It demolishes the power of death! Death was unable to hold back such power because it was not superficial! Jesus arose in victory beloved and all power was given to Him! Oh, they've been searching for ways to disprove this great event, yet, without controversy, even the world was in darkness, the very nature bowed in reverence to the eternal God of the universe! When Jesus rose my friends, *"Death Was Swallowed Up in Victory!"* Even the very wind felt its impact!

God is bigger, He's advance, more sophisticated and highly knowledgeable than the technological breakthrough of today! When God said, "let there be light,"[45] all he had to do was speak it into existence because, even nature itself was subjected to His command! David said: "The earth is the Lord's and the fullness thereof; the world, and they that dwell therein. For He had founded it upon the seas, and established it upon the floods. Who shall ascend into the hill of the Lord?

---

[44] Power (Greek)
[45] Genesis 1.3

Or who shall stand in his holy place?"[46] David went further: "The heavens declare the glory of God; and the firmament sheweth his handywork. Day unto day uttereth speech, and night unto night sheweth knowledge."[47] We recognizes that it's only a God who is superior to nature can speak to a raging sea and the sea obeyed His voice! Man began an exploration, they have gotten some breakthrough going to the moon, now they are researching for a pathway to travel to Mars, yet Jesus need not looking for a breakthrough into space because He Himself is in total control of space. He places the sun into its orbit, the moon is firmly fitted together by His power and the entire cosmos, is all a display of a God that is intelligent and greatly the designer of them all!

"For by him were all things created, that are in heaven, and that are in earth, visible and invisible, whether they be thrones, or dominions, or principalities, or powers: all things were created by him, and for him: And he is before all things, and by him all things consist. And he is the head of the body, the church: who is the beginning, the firstborn from the dead; that in all things he might have the preeminence. For it pleased the Father that in him should all fulness dwell; And, having made peace through the blood of his cross, by him to reconcile all things unto himself; by him, I say, whether they be things in earth, or things in heaven."[48]

Jesus left His throne in glory, came to planet Earth, went down into hell and many saw Him transfigured before their eyes, he went on back to glory and space and time is directed and controlled by Him! Oh yes, "All things were made by him; and without him was not anything made that

---

[46] Psalms 24.1-3
[47] Psalms 19.1-2
[48] Colossians 1.16-20

was made. In him was life; and the life was the light of men. And the light shineth in darkness; and the darkness comprehended it not!"[49]

Considering this great God am talking about, He did not need a computer monitor to figure out how he could stop the bleeding of a woman whose condition was going out of control, she was healed only by the power of a simple touch of His garment! God does not need a research lab that will enable Him to find a cure for the man that was born blind. The greatest ophthalmologist to have ever lived is Jesus! He took some dirt into His hands, then He spit on the dirt and anointed the eyes, then told the blind man, go wash your eyes, then immediately his eyes were opened! What advisor does God need to call the dead back to life? All that the Lord did was call out the name, Lazarus come forth!

See, while we are busy reading each sentence, the God we serve had already closed the book, in fact, God new every detail of the book before it was written! That's why to those that are sick and in need of a physician, there's a great doctor, the balm in Gilead. He specializes in top grade medicine made from His own blood. He can heal any sickness without an examination. The greatest heart surgeon sitting on His operating table, you will realize His skills are superior to all doctors of the world. Your mind needs realignment? Call this man! If you're dead or at the point of death, you can call Him just the same! You don't have to stand at the pool waiting, because now that the water is troubled, you can just step right in. Your condition is not beyond God's reach, thirty eight years are not too long for God to act, and His power is within reach!

---

[49] John 1.3-5

Maybe you've been suffering with diabetes for a long time and you think it's impossible for you to receive the healing you've sought but, the God that deals effectively with blood is available! Oh, you're told the cancer in your body is getting out of control, but remember Jesus is still touched with the feelings of your infirmities! I can understand that you've been plagued with the AIDS virus and you feel as though life is over for you, well I want to tell you that Christ our Lord is the author of red and white blood cells, He can transform every cells in your body not next week, but today, right now His power is within reach! He can speak to that condition, He'll breathe in that condition and He'll give just a simple touch in and through the very core of that body and you'll experience an everlasting change! Oh yes, Jesus is only a touch away! God is bigger than that problem in your stomach, just one droplet of His blood will penetrate that area even now! He's got a brand new liver for you if you will touch Him by faith! The water is trouble, all you should do now is step in by faith, and the mountains of your situation can be removed today! There is a Holy Ghost lazier with the anointing power to cut deep at the very root and let me tell you something, not a trace of infection will be left! Can you feel the burning sensation flowing through your body? It is God that's doing a wonderful work even now! By faith I want you to claim it, accept it right now! Push down on that burning, push down on that heat, it is God doing an operation, He's cutting away some stuff right now! Praise Him, Praise Him!

A 30-Day Devotional

Day One

It Was All For Me

Scripture Reading: Romans 5: 1-8
Key Verse: Romans 5: 8

"But God commendeth his love toward us, in that, while we were yet sinners, Christ died for us."

Now that we have obtained favor with God, we have come into a great legacy, we are blessed with great wealth that the world can never destroy. There is a love that is priceless, one that is untouchable! There is yet someone available to those whose hearts have be broken and is now seeking a real, true love, the invitation is open to come in and invest into this great and impressive plan. Here we find in this life we might have to work all our life to impress someone that you thought might have loved you yet, this love God have for you and me, while we were yet sinners, the Bible said, "Christ died for you!" Oh, what an excitement! Christ died for me! Really, can you imagine, can you picture your level of peculiarity? For God's only son to die for you even when you were stained in sin, then that means you are profoundly special! When one is actually living uprightly, just maybe one person would be dedicated to your cause and died on your behalf, but to be filthy, wretched and undone! Only the Lord Jesus would consider us to be anything worthwhile. You've seen already the way folks treated individuals for an error, turning their backs but in sin, they are deemed special because Christ died for us, yes there is someone on our side that really cares! One that won't condemn us, It worth shouting! The bible said, every good gifts and every perfect gift comes from God. Good gifts are to be treasured and the greatest gift which one can ever gain is found in Jesus Christ. This should be a gift to be treasured. Glory to God! It was love why Jesus bought grace through His blood. God commendeth His love! Yes, it was love why Jesus died, loving sinners so much and dying for them, opening up the way for salvation that anyone that actually calls upon Him, shall be saved! Grace is important to you, grace in your home, right at your disposal, receive this gift today, the unmerited favor of God. Today, there is no greater love than that a man should lay down his life for a friend. You are a friend of the Lord, claim this gift, it belongs to you, praise the Lord!

Prayer:

Lord, I'm thankful to be called your friend. I commit to you all my affairs, humbling myself before you. Thanks for the grace you've given. Amen!

Day Two

The Spotless Lamb of God

Scripture Reading John 1: 23 - 37
Key Verse John 1: 36

*"And looking upon Jesus as he walked,
He saith, behold the Lamb of God!"*

    In the book of Isaiah chapter forty verse three (40: 3), here was one of the greatest prophesy from the prophet Isaiah in the Old Testament, which the Apostle John in the New Testament revealed prophetically, as he saw the Messiah, Jesus Christ approaching. Here he boldly declared, "Behold the Lamb of God!" There are certain characteristics of a lamb. One that stands out is that he is humble. This is what Jesus represents, humility. The Lord came to us as a humble lamb, taking on himself all the sins of humanity. How did John know that this-was in fact the "Spotless Lamb? When you are able to recognize that you are a sinner. You will see Jesus as John declares Him, "The Lamb that takes away the sins of the World." It is true that many after witnessing the power of John they concluded he was in fact the Christ. John declared to the people, "I may possess the anointing to do great things, yet, I am not the one, there cometh one after me whose shoes am not worthy to unloose!" He was thus the forerunner of Christ, preparing a straight path for the Master Jesus. To truly recognize Jesus, you must have a personal relationship with Him. How is your relationship with the Lord today? Is he really the spotless lamb that have cleansed you from your sin? It's very easy to acknowledge knowing someone through identity, but to truly know Christ, you must get wrapped up into His word, get into the spirit because if you do not know Him through the spirit then you really do not know Him! John said, I baptize with water, but one standeth among you, whom ye know not. I believe that by this time in history, there are many that can testify that they know the one we preach, His Name is Jesus! Jesus is the sin taker! If today you are struggling in your sins, trust Jesus, oh, you'll never be the same. Come to the Savior, he patiently wait, come bring your problems and cares, come he is ready with mercy and grace, Jesus is pleading why wait?

Prayer:

Lord, we celebrate you today. You are the forgiver of sins. Take all my sin and wash me right now. Make me completely whole. Amen!

Day Three

℘

God Gave You His Best

Scripture Reading: Romans 3: 21-31
Key Verse: Romans 3: 24

*"Being justified freely by His grace through
the redemption that is in Christ Jesus"*

All over the world, people are trying to obtain some level of holiness and salvation by simply offering services. In general, they are of the impression that if they render some good deeds in the community and to those around them, then they are qualified to receive eternal life with Jesus. It was true then that no one could actually convince those Pharisees that were of this notion, they were righteous by simply following the law. We know that the gift of grace through redemption that is in Jesus, is all it takes to justify man from sin and this is all that qualifies us, not by works! True salvation only comes through the grace of the Almighty God. The finish work of Christ which He accomplishes at the cross, the very act of grace could never be possible if Jesus hadn't been to the cross. He went all the way for us, but for the joy that was set before Him, He endured the cross, despising the shame! Having put our faith in this great provision, Paul said, we are justified freely by His grace through the redemption that is in Christ Jesus. He gave us the very best! You cannot purchase this, you cannot Work to obtain this. Paul went further and states clearly, for by grace are ye saved through faith, not by works least any man should boast. You are free from sin, justified, having obtained redemption that is in Christ. You are indeed brought with a price, oh it was the precious blood of Christ that paid the penalty once and for all! Now you can say like Paul, there is therefore now, no condemnation to them that are in Christ Jesus. Old things have passed away and behold all things have become new!

Prayer:

Lord you have provided the best way for my salvation, I am saved and thankful for this great gift of salvation. I praise you, I honor you. Amen!

Day Four

You Can Enter at an Open Invitation

Scripture Reading Mark 15: 33-41
Key Verse Mark 15: 37, 38

"And Jesus cried with a loud voice and gave up the ghost, and the veil of the temple was rent in twain from the top to the bottom."

One of history's most remarkable moment was the day of the crucifixion of Christ. His death was of such peculiarity, not only that the veil of the temple was rent but that there was darkness, the sun was darkened over all the earth. The truth is that Christ death did not affect only humanity, but nature itself was moved emotionally at the death of the Lord! Yes, the whole foundation of the world was affected! Imagine His loud cry on the cross as they nailed Him, as they beat and spat on Him, it was cruel, brutal and inhumane. Yet by his death, the gift of salvation was the instant result. The veil was rent, you and I had obtained access to enter boldly before the throne. You can bring before the Lord all your cares and brokenness by yourself because the wonderful Savior Jesus Christ has died for you! He has taken the penalty, your curses and on Himself borne all your sorrows. This great opportunity, to having now this great knowledge of His death and to have knowledge that this is what had brought transformation to many lives. You are to rejoice in having a High Priest, whose name is JESUS CHRIST our Lord! He intercedes on your behalf. He gives comfort to the faint and He's touched with the feelings of your infirmities. As in the song: *"What can wash away my sins, nothing but the blood of Jesus, what can make me whole again, nothing but the blood of Jesus. Oh precious is the fount that makes me white as snow, no other fount I know, nothing but the blood of Jesus,"* the blood of Jesus, is indeed the only remedy to cleanse a guilty sinner, you and me. There is an open invitation to all, just to enter in and receive permanent forgiveness because the veil of the temple was rent and you and I have freedom to enter boldly at the throne.

Prayer:

Heavenly Father, we thank you today for the kind provision you have made to us, sending Jesus to be our savior. Thanks for the unblemished lamb and we receive the salvation given through his name. Amen!

Day Five

What a Great Easter!

Scripture Reading Isaiah 53: 1-12
Key Verse Isaiah 53: 6

"All we like sheep have gone astray. We have turned everyone to his own way. And the Lord had laid on him the iniquity of us all."

Do you like the Easter bunny? For this Easter, we have the opportunity to celebrate a lamb! What, Celebrate a lamb, shouldn't we eat a lamb? The lamb in which we celebrate is Jesus, this will be the best Easter for us! A lamb sacrificed and he's now the Shepherd, the Bishop of our souls. Today, Jesus is risen and we that have strayed, have lost our way in sin. Christ the Lord of glory has risen and we can carry all our sins and laid them all on Him. There was a severe curse on humanity when Adam sinned and man were destined to die because sin had gotten so prevalent, God had to destroy Sodom and Gomorrah yet, man still would not repent. In spite of it all God love us so much that He still provided a way that we can receive salvation and Eternal life. This great Easter morning, Mary went to the tomb that they laid our Lord, she was asked, who are you seeking, the living among the dead? He is not here, He is risen, come see the place where He was laid! What joy beloved, what excitement! What comfort, our Lord is not here, He is risen! He is not dead, death is swallowed up in victory! Because of the risen Lord and Savior, our gift of salvation has been born and we have this Wonderful hope that we too will rise to meet the Lord on the great Resurrection.

Prayer:

Lord, we hail you King of kings, and Lord of Lords. Today and forever thank you for the finished work at the cross. Thanks for shedding your precious blood for a sinner such as me. I bless you today, you alone are worthy. Amen!

Day Six

What Great Awe in His Presence!

Scripture Reading Ex. 34: 1-9
Key Verse Ex. 34:8

"And Moses made haste, and bowed his head towards the earth, and worshipped."

Worshipping God must be a life style, this act must be done without constraint. How one could refuse to worship God after all that He has done. When you witnessed God's magnificent greatness, when you view His overall power, His might and His glorious splendor, your love and admiration for Him would allow you to bow in His presence and worship the Almighty King of glory! Oh! He's worthy to be praise, from the rising of the sun to it's going down thereof! Moses at the backside of the desert saw the mighty acts of the true and living God. He saw the demonstration of his power on Mount Sinai in the burning bush, God spoke to him and gave him the commandments and that even in the desert, the Wonders of God was not even hidden. When you actually heard the wonderful voice of God speaking, then you saw that He appears in the cloud, Moses bowed and worship! What will it take for you to fall on your face and worship God? He's still speaking in the clouds, He's still in the deserts and He's still in the mountains! God do you really see in me something worthwhile to be used by you? He made haste, Lord I won't even wait, the presence of the Lord is just awesome! Moses Wanted to enjoy the awe of God! Beloved, once you sensed God's presence, He don't need to always showing up in person, but like He descended in the clouds and stood with Moses, you must be moved to worship Him because He is God and because He is God and He dwells and inhabits our praise our worship is a sweet aroma, sweet smelling savor in His nostrils. Can you imagine worshipping God right now and letting Him come and dwell tight there with you, in the very midst of your situation you are offering them up in worship and the God of Heaven, sits with you pouring comfort, granting peace, filling you with His power! Oh, you can reason with Him like Moses, if now I have found grace in Thy sight, oh Lord I pray Thee, go among us! Go before us God and we know that we'll be secure.

Prayer:

Lord, help us to see the need and importance of worship. When we come before you Oh God. Help us to pour out ourselves that our worship will be sweet. And that you'll come and dwell in our presence, Amen.

Day Seven

Heaven Will Not Be Silent

Scripture Reading Matt. 27: 45~56
Key Verse Matt. 27: 52

"And the graves were opened, and many bodies of the saints which slept arose."

The death of Christ was not just an ordinary death, in fact, the result of His death did not just caused a stir in Jerusalem, at Calvary, and His death had a universal impact! Every fabric of society, the entire Heaven's, the World on a whole was in some way giving glory and honor and celebrating this historical event. Heaven was impacted, earth and all of nature was moved at the death of Christ. No ordinary man, no king, no president or even the greatest military leader could die, and like Christ cause such a great reaction. There were great earthquakes, darkness which covers the whole earth, the earth became still, yes, she came to attention because somehow, she knew that something had happen to the King of glory that was strange and even the very element of the world could not contain itself! The very nature was petrified at the death of Christ. The bible said, graves were opened and dead bodies of the saints were risen up, am talking about events that precedes the resurrection. There was a great wonder over the land, it was undoubtedly the wonderful power of His Majesty! What a great power and awe in the name of Jesus? It baffles the mind, oh, it's mind boggling! You see friends, the death of Christ truly means change. While other great men died without incidents, the son of God died and Heaven would not be silent, he died to bring reconciliation, he'll bring back that union, that fellowship between God and man, salvation, eternal life, hope and peace. We can all proclaim that, power belongs to God, the Eternal Lamb that was slain. His death causes you and me to live and we rejoice in the fact that He's not dead any more, He's alive, death was swallowed up in victory!

Prayer:

Lord, I thank you for dying on the cross for me. You paid the price for my sins. Help me today to walk in your righteousness and to tell others that you alone are Lord, Amen.

Day Eight

☙

Alleluia, We've Have a Savior

Scripture Reading Isa. 9: 1-7
Key Verse Isa. 9:6

"For unto us a child is born, unto us a son is given: and the government shall be upon his shoulder: and his name shall be called Wonderful, Counsellor, The mighty God, The everlasting Father, The Prince of Peace."

The whole idea of a child born into a family is one of joy and celebration. Once it is found out that a child is expected there it is usually followed with great expectation. We find also the anxiety and curiosity of the gender only to determine what special gift to choose so that family and friends can flood him or her with gifts. The prophet Isaiah had prophesied the birth of the most awaited Messiah who was to be born. He even went further describing some of the many roles and responsibilities of this child. He will be a Son! He will be responsible for government and there are great significance to the names given to Him. Isaiah said His name shall be called IMMANUEL, interpreted "God with us." A divine person born to us as a Son, how very unique? His name shall be called, Wonderful, His name here implies, wonder, marvelous things will happen from this Son, things that are too high to articulate in the natural mind! He's the Counselor, to resolve, to deliberate, to guide, to devise. In fact, you can consult him because he is the greatest adviser. A know all things advisor! He is the Mighty God, you cannot get anything bigger than that, He's mighty to the utmost! So mighty in battle, mighty to the pulling down of strongholds!

Mighty worrier, Almighty! The Everlasting Father, this Son will be forever, from everlasting to everlasting, there will be no end to His government! Forever you can consult with Him and forever you'll see the demonstration of His power. The Prince of Peace, He will be the complete head, the chief, the captain forever! This son, God hath highly exalted Him and given Him a name that is above every name, that at the Name of Jesus every knee shall bow and every tongue shall confess that Jesus Christ is Lord! As you look and seek the direction of our Savior, let's understand that this Lord and Savior, is truly the best friend to have. Alleluia!

Prayer:

God, we rejoice in the fact that we have a Savior, the blessed Son Jesus Christ. We bless you and worship you, and we honor you today, Amen.

Day Nine

૭⌒

A Settled Peace Beyond Measure

Scripture Reading John 14: 26- 31
Key Verse John 14: 27

"Peace I leave with you, my peace I give unto you: not as the world giveth, give I unto you. Let not your heart be troubled, neither let it be afraid."

When we consider the word of God and how it comforts us, we are certain that God's word is something rather bigger than we can ever imagine. Our Lord Jesus Christ is really our peace! Oh yes, He said it, my peace I leave with you, my peace I give you. What peace can one find in the world, especially in today's world? Nothing but an empty promise, yet, the Lord Jesus Christ gives comfort and reassurance, "let not your heart be troubled, neither let it be afraid!" The giver of peace, the one that passes all human understanding told His disciples, it is expedient that I go, because if I go I will send you the Comforter, I will send you the Holy Ghost! The Holy Ghost will be your guiding light, He will be the compass that you need. He will be the shade and the very peace that the world cannot give! This is why it's so very important that we dispatch to all that we encounter in this life a taste of this peace that we receive from God, then the world will become a much better place. Christ the blessed hope of Glory, dwelling on in the inside, thus you reflect even that same peace on the outside! Will you be the agent of peace to your community today? Will you be willing to share God's peace to others? It is beautiful, it is rewarding, it is fulfilling. Now that you are blessed with this peace, you must live your life as though you are really a disciple of Christ, demonstrating to others the abundant peace of the Lord. Encouraging others whose hearts are troubled, let not your heart be troubled, beloved, neither let it be afraid because you are serving and trusting the True and Living God!

Prayer:

Lord, help me to be that instrument of your peace, let me share the love to all. The love that was shed abroad in my heart. I want others to see you reflecting through me. Thanks for being my peace today, Amen.

Day Ten

Is There Something Wrong With Me?

Scripture Reading Gen. 6: 1-8
Key Verse Gen. 6: 6

"And it repented the Lord that he had made man on the earth, and it grieved him at his heart."

When God created man as we read in the book of Genesis, His plan was a beautiful one, this was ideally for us to live righteously in a world of paradise. When man did evil and disobeyed God as in the case of Adam and Eve in the Garden of Eden, this was very tragic, because man loses out on such wonderful plan and suffers because of such evil. Imagine such plan yet man would turn to sinning in such a terrible way, which had actually grieved God. Today, however, we don't have to worry because we have Jesus, the one that who is provided grace on our behalf. Now in the place of sin we have an opportunity to receive pardon. Today we are to live our lives for the sole purpose to please God. Are you tired of bringing shame and dishonor to the God who made you? The Bible said, there's a way that seem right unto a man but at the end thereof is death. We no longer should live in disobedience but, to trust in God's grace and forgiveness so that God can relent judgment and pour his forgiveness upon us. May God help us today to change the course of our lives and see him move in a powerful way.

Prayer:

Father I am sorry for my often hurt and dishonor you. I trample on your grace and am sorry, help me live for you. Amen.

Day Eleven

A Life Honored By God

Scripture Reading Proverbs 15: 1-9
Key Verse Proverbs 14:34

"Righteousness exalteth a nation: but sin is a reproach to any people."

The Nation and the world at large (for some very strange reasons) had drifted away from its core values and principles which once was at the center piece and at the very fabric of our existence. Our attitude to honoring God and abiding by His words especially those that are leading His people have been ingrained in our lives from the very beginning. Overtime, we've seen the severe damage caused by unrighteous governing something detrimentally puts at risk a future secure and well pleasing to the Almighty God. Solomon new well what it was to lead in righteousness and in his incapability to the extent of leading the people of God, he earnestly request wisdom from God. In your own natural ability, God's plans will be destroyed and Solomon new that in order to prosper in the things of God, you need His wisdom richly. It is true that you will be exalted once operating in the righteousness of God. Once we refuses to act righteously and or in the fear of God, we are deemed to fail miserable. Solomon said it best, he said in essence "sin is a reproach to any people, it will ultimately cause you pain and hurt, it will allow your life to be cut short, it will bring much shame and discontent to your life and loved ones!"

You can never prosper when taking sin's approach, nor can you reach a viable place in God because the simple truth is, God will not dwell in the tents of the wicked. A life honored by God is one operated in righteousness.

Prayer:

Father, please show us how to govern our family in righteousness, we understand that's the only way we can truly prosper, help us to forever seek your wisdom for this we pray, Amen.

Day Twelve

Nothing Matters Like Jesus

Scripture Reading Proverbs 14:1-13
Key verse Proverbs 14:13

"Even in laughter the heart is sorrowful; and the end of that mirth is heaviness."

It's amazing that one can be laughing, he might seem to be reflecting fun outwardly, yet deep down on the inside he is suffering great wounds. People's lives are filled with grief and sorrow in a world filled with gloom and despair. Looking around us today, our hearts have burned within us observing the many hurts and pains experienced through this great economic upheaval. Yes, the severity of this financial crisis is undoubtedly taking a serious toll on countless souls, heaping up insurmountable burdens on family, creating broken homes an added increase in divorce among so many tragic issues in the lives of families and friends. Today for many, instead of a smile, many are left with a frown. We realized through the spirit and the Word of God however, that nothing can bring true satisfaction like knowing Jesus and receiving Him as our Savior and Lord. The void and emptiness we feel can only be replaced with a touch from Him that understands our pains. Only once we relinquish all our cares and situations to Him then and only then can, we turn into true laughter and smile again. That's the only way for us to smell the sweet aroma of peace. Yes, even in very difficult conditions Christ can make a difference erasing the pains from your life.

Prayer:

Oh God, you know it hurts real bad, We can't even talk about it too much we bring our life and condition to you, please change the existing condition and turn things around. Do for us a miracle, we need it today, Amen.

Day Thirteen

Have You Felt His Presence?

Scripture Reading Prov. 15:26-33
Key verse Prov. 15:29

"The Lord is far from the wicked: but he hearth the prayer of the righteous."

    Oh! It's truly a great feeling knowing that the Lord is near to me. It even feels better that He hears me when I pray. There are many great benefits that we reap when we are called children of God. When we've taken on the Son of God, Jesus Christ as our Lord and Savior, our prayers are heard by God and we can feel His very presence knowing He's with us. The fact is clear, as you see those that are wicked and hate God, know this, God is far from them and what a terrible state to find one self, been hated by God? When God is far from you, you are in serious trouble. There you have no covering, no shelter, no assurance, because the wicked are not covered by God. However, with all certainty, God, our Lord, He is over the righteous and more so, His ears are attentive to their cries! Now this means you should be dancing, yes, you should be rejoicing saints of God! What a great consolation that we have in God, we don't have to worry and become envious at the prosperity of the wicked because their prosperity are only for a while. We are confident that our eternal destiny are secure, better yet, we have an abundance of His grace and all things that we need will be supplied by the God who cares for His people. Today, let us keep our focus on the Lord knowing that He's very near to you.

Prayer:

Lord we thank you for the security we have in you, help us not to drift from your covering but to continue to trust you Amen."

Day Fourteen

☙

Adapting Self-Control

Scripture Reading Proverbs 16: 22-33
Key Verse Proverbs 16:32

"He that is slow to anger is better than the mighty; and he that ruleth his spirit than he that taketh a city."

Solomon said: "Anger rests in the bosom of the fool." There seem to be a spirit of anger which is now sweeping the land. Sin is the most contributing factor behind this anger. The enemy uses such strong device to trap us and while we may never look at it this way before, God calls us when we operate in anger, we are classified as fools! How long will we continue with a behavior as though we are fools'? We must understand that it's time for us to turn to God and start to function in a way that God will see us living according to His spirit. While fathers are angry looking at their children drifting away from family values. Mothers are equally angry because of the burdens and pressures of life, children are very angry because of their surroundings. It's a time when we as a people must come to the place when we practice self-control which is the actual desire that God have for our live. We can't afford to bite and devour each other. Cain killed his brother Able and we must get reed of the Cain like spirit in our lives. If we would turn to loving again as we ought to, we'll find that life for us will be more productive, more resourceful and rewarding. Let us follow hard the passage of scripture and be slow to anger, slow to wrath and understand that we will be better than the mighty when love is the tool that is used in place of anger and bitterness. Let us manage our spirit well and listen to the voice of God as he speaks, that He will be glorified in us and our future will be bright.

Prayer:

Father you have made us to love, forgive us for failing you, for being so angry which constantly causes pain. Help us to look to you for the direction that is needed in emotional conflicts that our actions will bless others and not to hurt. Amen.

Day Fifteen

☙

Make It Up With Your Brother

Scripture Reading Gen. 33: 1-5
Key Verse Gen. 33: 4

"And Esau ran to meet him, and embraced him, and fell on his neck, and kissed him: and they wept."

    We often heard the term, "blood is thicker than water." It's an analogy used to show a close connection, a common bond and a kind of loyalty among family! However, because of the blood of Jesus, we are really "thicker" and that's why we can run to Him with our often problems and this thickness means He'll never rejects us. There appears to be a major conflict with two brothers, Jacob and Esau. Pass hurts and disloyalty can cause a life time of separation a separation that can take many decade to reconcile. Truthfully, family should never live that way it is very heart wrenching. Why is making up so very hard to do? Two sons came from the same womb, in fact, twins. This is exactly what the enemy wants to do, he wants to create situations so that the unity and love can be distorted. There were jealousy, bitter envy, a boiling range which was whacking havoc in this family. Family can encounter very difficult situations that might somehow cause strains. These severe confrontations can rip family apart. It is possible that you might not suffer the same situation like Esau and Jacob, but somehow things between you and your family might not be completely whole. When will you decide to make it up, will you do it today? Regardless of what the problems may be, follow the pattern of Esau and Jacob, Esau ran to meet Jacob and embraced him and fell on his neck and kissed him and they wept! Blood is thicker than water! What you are waiting on, you should not wait until next year, it means today! As the opportunity presents itself, you must do it as you have the time. Your brother, your sister, you haven't communicated in a long time, make it up today. It's not that bad, you are from the same womb, your mother's son, your mother's daughter! Make this a new beginning, start over, erase that old passed as Esau with his brother Jacob, and make that call, kiss and embrace and let the Lord be praised.

Prayer:

Father, show me how to unite with my loved ones. You have taught us that unity is strength. I want to be the peacemaker you have created me to be. Let me be that example today, Amen!

Day Sixteen

෩

Such a Bad Perception

Scripture Reading Gen. 33: 1-4
Key Verse Gen. 33: 1

"And Jacob lifted up his eyes, and looked, and, behold, Esau came, and with him four hundred men. And he divided the children unto Leah, and unto Rachel, and unto the two handmaids."

    One may never able to predict the way in which the Lord will work in certain situations we face. We can never question God approach, why is He's using such strategy or why is He taking this route simple when God is at work we'll be amazed at the outcome and yes, it will ultimately work out for our good. Beloved, when God is at work on your behalf, everything that concerns your life, He will work them out for His glory! Why should you second guess God's ability to working out a better plan? He is God, He knows all things better, in fact, best! God said that he will make your enemies be at peace with you. How will that happen? Well, He said it and all you must do is believe it! Oh well, God, how will this be possible? Trust Him, nothing is impossible with God. Jacob saw his brother coming with four hundred men, his natural perception was "my brother was coming to destroy me." Human tendency is always to begin with a negative view. Don't you believe that people are repentant? Don't you think that God is still changing lives? Yes, Esau was a dangerous man, yet it's true that God is able to change the hearts of men. God had already touched Esau's heart and fill him with love and compassion and his only motive was an expression of peace, that which only God was capable of giving! How is your heart today? Can you see things in a positive light as you are serving the Lord? Try not to place yourself under unnecessary pressure and began to worry when the Lord is bringing to you the blessing that you need. Watch out, your enemies are coming not to hurt or harm you, but to bring peace and reconciliation!

The God in whom you're trusting will not allow the enemies to destroy you, relax, stay calm, stand still, what you're seeing at the moment is really not what it is because God is at work in the hearts of those that are rising up against you and you will be the victor and not the victim!

Prayer:

Lord, my life is in your hand, my family, their lives are in your hand. Touch hearts today and make them tender. Bring peace in the midst of all the storms of life. Help us to face our problems without fear, knowing that we are in your hands, Amen.

Day Seventeen

Be Not Afraid, Only Pray

Scripture Reading Gen. 32: 1-8
Key Verse Gen. 32: 7

"Then Jacob was greatly afraid and distressed: and he divided the people that was with him, and the flocks, and herds, and the camels, into two bands."

Prayer is indeed the Christians most explosive and most accessible weapon. This Weapon when used correctly will cause an explosion! In difficult times when we are faced with danger, this weapon should be our security even when running, we can be shooting this Weapon. Why did our fathers accomplish many victories? They have constantly practiced dispatching their weapons effectively and the results they received were good. See friends, the enemies cannot stand it when the people of God began to pray. For the weapon of our warfare are not carnal but mighty through God to the pulling down of stronghold! You have a live weapon in this war and it is prayer in the Name of Jesus! Are you at a very distressing place in your spirit? Then pray! Jacob found himself at this place, a place of distress, and at this sad place, he wanted to do things the way they appears. In your own eyes, the devil wants you to forget that there is a God when faced with your hard trials. In your trials, the God of Heaven will be available to you especially when you learn to call out His name. Your immediate condition is only temporary, He will reveal Himself even in distress! God came to Jacob in the dark, will you recognize the Lord as He's working on your behalf, even in your dark tunnels?

Jacob took the opportunity and he wrestled with God. I will not let you go until you bless me! You cannot allow your hurts and emotional breakdown to keep you bound to the point that you cannot reach out and touch God. Forget your problems today and do some wrestling, hold on firmly to the Lord of glory, take you a firm grip, be determine not to let go of the Lord. Call unto me, and I will answer thee, and show thee great and mighty things, which thou knowest not.[50]

Prayer:

Lord, I present to you all my fears, my distresses and all my regrets. As I take a firm grip on you today. Hear me and act now on my behalf. Place in me the power and strength that I need to stand and let ne ever continue trusting in your grace, Amen.

---

[50] Jeremiah 33: 3

Day Eighteen

He Came For a Purpose

Scripture Reading Luke 2: 1-7
Key Verse Luke 2: 7

"And she brought forth her firstborn son, and wrapped him in swaddling clothes, and laid him in a manger; because there was no room for them in the inn."

Have you ever paused and imagine what the condition of this world would be without this wonderful gift to mankind, the blessed baby Jesus'? Joy to the world the Lord has come! Undoubtedly, the Lord Jesus Christ truly makes a difference because He is the loving Savior of the world. Looking at the condition of men, it is true we are all lost without having a true Shepherd. To us, Jesus came for a greater purpose, born of a virgin, meek and lowly. Today, the poor, the weak and those without hope are blessed with a future because of this first born Son. We often question the power and mysteries of our Great and Mighty God yet, because of His love for humanity, He made provisions for us. He foresees the sinful condition of the human race and He knew that none were perfect enough to provide the way to reconcile us back to God. Therefore by His great power, God places Himself into a virgin, conceived by the Holy Ghost. How did that happened? The great mystery of God is not for us all to know in detail, for there is nothing impossible with God, we should only trust Him! The bible said, she brought forth her first born Son, wrapped Him in swaddling clothes and laid Him in a manger! This might Sound like poverty to me or to you, but let's not be fooled harboring such notion, everything in this world belongs to God including all palace, the mansions and every fine places to live they are indeed belongs to Him. Christ came to redeem the poor, and for this purpose He came, to seek and to save that which was lost!

He came to preach the gospel to the poor, to heal the brokenhearted, to preach deliverance to the captives and recovering of sight to the blind, to set at liberty them that are bruised.[51] Let this Christ be yours today.

Prayer:

Father, we thank you for sending your Son as a special gift to us, Amen.

---

[51] Luke 4: 18

Day Nineteen

It Was All For Me

Scripture Reading Romans 5: 1-8
Key Verse Romans 5: 8

"But God commendeth his love toward us, in that, while we were yet sinners, Christ died for us."

Now that we have obtained such wonderful favor from God, we have come into a legacy so great and a divine wealth the world cannot destroy. There is a priceless love, a love unique and untouchable! It is a love that those whose hearts have be broken and is now seeking a real true love can come into this great legacy. It is true that in this life one might have to work all his natural life seeking to impress someone that you'd think to have loved you yet, this love that God had given, it is one that, "while we were yet sinners, the Christ of Glory, died for us! Oh, can you really fathom your peculiarity? It takes the only Son of God to die for us even when we were stain in sin, even when we were slaves to sin, indeed you and I are special! Well you are living the righteous life, one might die for you, but to be filthy, wretched and undone! Only the Lord would consider you to be something. You've seen how folks mistreat individuals for their simple errors, turning their backs on them, but Glory be to God! In sin, you are deemed special because Christ even went far to die for you. Are you glad that there is someone on your side that really care! It worth shouting! The bible said, every good gifts and every perfect gift comes from God. Good gifts are to be treasured and of these great gifts, the gift of salvation is found in Jesus and we treasured this special gift today, glory to God. It was love why Jesus sends Grace, God commendeth His love!

Yes it is love why Jesus died, loving sinners so much dying and opening up the way for salvation that anyone that actually call upon Him, the Name of the Lord Jesus, shall be saved! Grace is important to you, in your home, right at your disposal.

Today, there is no greater love than that a man should lay down his life for a friend. You are a friend of the Lord, claim this gift, it belongs to you, praise the Lord!

Prayer:

I Lord, am thankful to be called your friend. I commit to you all my affairs. Humbling myself before you. Thanks for the grace you've given, Amen.

Day Twenty

හ

The Spotless Lamb of God

Scripture Reading John 1: 23 - 37
Key Verse John 1: 36

"And looking upon Jesus as he walked, he saith,
Behold the Lamb of God!"

In the book of Isaiah chapter 40 verse 3, here was one of the greatest prophesy told in scripture. The prophet Isaiah in the Old Testament, which the Apostle John in the New Testament revealed prophetically, as he saw the Messiah, Jesus Christ approaching. Here he declared, "Behold the Lamb of God!"[52] There are certain characteristics of lamb. One that is evident, is this, that he is humble this is Jesus' nature, "humble." The Lord came to us as a humble lamb, taking on himself all the sins of humanity. How did John new this was in fact the "Spotless Lamb? You must be able to recognize the Lord as you discover that your sins are taken away. John could identify this Lamb, Jesus Christ from a distant! It is true that John possessed some traits of power within himself that those people around him could notice. After witnessing this power many thought John was in fact the Christ, but he declared: "I am not the one, there cometh one after me whose shoes am not worthy to unloose!"[53] He was thus the forerunner of Christ, preparing a straight path for the Master Jesus. Beloved, to truly recognize Jesus, you must have a personal relationship with Him. How is your

---

[52] John 1.36
[53] Translation mine.

relationship with the Lord today? Is He really the Spotless Lamb that have cleansed you from your sin? It's very easy to acknowledge knowing someone through identity, but to truly know Christ, you must get wrapped up into His word, get into the spirit because if you do not know Him through the spirit then you really do not know Him! John said, "I baptize with water, but One standeth among you, whom ye know not."[54]

I believe that by this time in history, there are many that can testify that they know the One we preach, His Name is Jesus! Jesus is the sin taker! If today you are struggling in your sins, trust Jesus, oh, you'll never be the same, come to the Savior, He patiently wait, come bring your problems and cares, come He is ready with mercy and grace, Jesus is pleading why wait?

Prayer:

Lord we celebrate you today. You are the forgiver of sins. Take all my sins and wash me right now. Make me completely whole. Amen!

---

[54] John 1.26

Day Twenty-One

God Gave You His Best

Scripture Reading Romans 3: 21-31
Key Verse Romans 3: 24

"Being justified freely by his grace through the redemption that is in Christ Jesus"

All over the world, people are trying to obtain salvation by simply offering services. In general, they feel that if they'll render some good deeds they are qualify to receive eternal life with Jesus. It was true then that no one could actually convinced those Pharisees that thought they were righteous by simply following the law. The gift of grace through redemption that is in Jesus is all that it takes to justify man from sin and this is all that qualifies us, not by works! True salvation only comes through the grace of the Almighty God. The finish work of Christ which he accomplished at the cross. The very act of grace could never be possible if Jesus hadn't been to the cross. He went all the way for us, but for the joy that was set before him, he endured the cross, despising the shame! Having put our faith in this great provision, Paul said, we are justified freely by his grace through the redemption that is in Christ Jesus. He gave us the very best! You cannot purchase this, you cannot work to obtain this. Paul went further and states clearly, for by grace are ye saved through faith, not by works least any man should boast. You are free from sin, justified, having obtained redemption that is in Christ. You are indeed brought with a price, oh it was the precious blood of Christ that paid the penalty once and for all! Now you can say like Paul, there is therefore now, no condemnation to them that are in Christ Jesus,[55] old things are passed away and behold all things are become new![56]

Prayer:

Lord you have provided the best way for my salvation. I am saved and I'm thankful for this great gift of salvation. I praise you, and I honor you. Amen!

---

[55] Romans 8.1
[56] 2 Corinthians 5.17

Day Twenty-Two

୫∂

You Can Enter at an Open Invitation

Scripture Reading Mark 15: 33-41
Key Verse Mark 15: 37-38

"And Jesus cried with a loud voice, and gave up the ghost. And the veil of the temple was rent in twain from the top to the bottom."

One of history's most remarkable moment was the crucifixion of Christ. His death was of such peculiarity, not only that the veil of the temple was rent but that there was darkness, the sun was darkened over all the earth. The truth is that Christ death did not affect only humanity, but nature itself was moved at the death of the Lord! Yes, the whole foundation of the world was moved in adoration to the King of Kings! Imagine His loud cry on the cross as they nailed Him, as they beat and spat on Him, it was cruel, brutal and inhumane. Yet by His death brought to man the gift of salvation which was an instant result. The veil was rent, you and I was given access to enter boldly before the throne. You can bring before the Lord all your cares and brokenness yourself because the wonderful Savior Jesus Christ has died for you! He has taken the penalty, your curses and on Himself borne all your sorrows. This great opportunity, having now this great knowledge of His death and to know that this is what brought transformation to many lives. You have a High Priest, His Name is JESUS! He intercedes on your behalf, He gives comfort to the faint and He's touched with the feelings of your infirmities. The song, what can wash away my sins, nothing but the blood of Jesus, what can make me whole again, n0thing but the blood of Jesus, oh precious is the fount that makes me while as snow, no other fo1mtI know, nothing but the blood of Jesus! The blood of Jesus, is indeed the only remedy to cleanse a guilty sinner. There is an open invitation to all, just to enter in and receive permanent forgiveness because the veil of the temple was rent and you and I have freedom to enter boldly at the throne.

Prayer:

Heavenly Father, we thank you today for the kind provision you have made to us sending Jesus to be our Savior. Thanks for the Salvation given through his name. Amen!

Day Twenty-Three

What a Great Easter!

Scripture Reading Isaiah 53: 1-12
Key Verse Isaiah 53: 6

"All we like sheep have gone astray; we have turned every one to his own way; and the Lord hath laid on him the iniquity of us all."

Do you like the Easter bunny? For this Easter, we have the opportunity to celebrate a lamb! "What, Celebrate a lamb, shouldn't we eat a lamb?" The lamb in which we celebrate is Jesus, this will be the best Easter for us! A Lamb sacrificed and he's now the Shepherd, the Bishop of our souls. Today, Jesus is risen and we that were going astray, lost our way in sin, Christ the Lord of glory has risen and we can carry all our sins and laid them all on Him. There was a severe curse on humanity when Adam sinned. Man were destined to die because sin had gotten so prevalent, God had to destroy Sodom and Gomorrah yet, man still would not repent. In spite of it all God loves us so much that He still provides for us a way that we can receive salvation. This great Easter morning, Mary went to the tomb that they laid our Lord, she was asked, who are you seeking, the living among the dead? He is not here, He is risen, come see the place where He was laid! What joy beloved, what excitement! What comfort, our Lord is not in the grave, He had risen! He is not dead, death is swallowed up in victory! Because of the risen Lord and Savior, our gift of salvation has been born and we have this wonderful hope that we too will rise to meet the Lord on the *Great Resurrection Morning*!

Prayer:

Lord, we hail you King of kings and Lord of lords today and forever. Thank you for the finished work on the cross. Thanks for shedding your precious blood for sinner such as me. I bless you today, you alone are worthy. Amen!

Day Twenty-Four

What Great Awe in His Presence!

Scripture Reading Ex. 34: 1-9
Key Verse Ex. 34:8

"And Moses made haste, and bowed his head toward the earth, and worshipped."

Worshipping God must be a life style, this act must be done without constraint. How could one refuse to worship God after all He has done? When you witnessed God's magnificent greatness, when you view His overall power, His might and His splendor, your love and admiration forces and reinforces you to bow before His presence and worship the Almighty King of glory! Oh! He's worthy to be praise, from the rising of the sun to it's going down thereof! Moses at the backside of the desert saw the mighty acts of the true and living God. He saw the demonstration of His power on Mount Sinai in the burning bush, God spoke to him and gave him the commandments and even in the desert, the wonders of God was not even hidden. When you actually heard the wonderful voice of God speaking, then you actually see that He appears in the cloud, Moses bowed and worship! What will it take for you to fall on your face and worship God? He's still speaking in the clouds, He's still in the deserts and He's still in the mountains! God do you really see in me something worthwhile to be used by you? He made haste, Lord I won't even wait, the presence of the Lord is just awesome! Moses wanted to enjoy the awe of God! Beloved, once you sensed God's presence, He don't need to always showing up in person, but like He descended in the clouds and stood with Moses, you must be moved to worship Him because He is God and He dwells and inhabits our praise and our worship is a sweet aroma, sweet smelling savor in His nostrils. Can you imagine worshipping God right now and watch Him come and dwell right there with you, in the very midst of your situation you are offering them up in worship and the God of Heaven, sits with you pouring comfort, granting peace, filling you with His power!

Oh, you can reason with Him like Moses, if now I have found grace in Thy sight, oh Lord I pray thee, go among us! Go before us, God and we know that we'll be secure.

Prayer:

Lord, help us to see the need and the importance of worship. When we come before you oh God, help us to pour out ourselves that our worship will be sweet and that you'll come and dwell in our presence, Amen!

Day Twenty-Five

Heaven Will Not Be Silent

Scripture Reading Matt. Z7: 45-56
Key Verse Matt. 27: 52

"And the graves were opened; and many bodies of the saints which slept arose."

The death of Christ was not just an ordinary death, in fact, the impact of His death could be felt in every fabric of the universe. Heaven was impacted, earth and all of nature was moved at the death of Christ. No ordinary man, a king, a president or even the greatest military leader will died like Christ and causes such great explosion. There were great earthquake, darkness which covers the whole earth, the earth became still, yes, and she came to attention because somehow, she knew that something had happen to the King of glory that was strange! Even the very nature was petrified at the death of Christ. The bible said, graves were opened and dead bodies of the saints were risen up, am talking about events that precede the resurrection. There was a great wonder over the land, it was undoubtedly the wonderful power of His majesty! What a great power that is in the name of Jesus? It baffles the mind, oh, it's mind boggling! You see friends, the death of Christ truly means change. While other great men died without incidents, the son of God died and Heaven would not be silent, He died to bring reconciliation, He'll bring back that union, that fellowship between God and man. All power belongs to God, the Lamb that was slain.

His death causes you and me to live and we rejoice in the fact that he's not dead any more, Jesus is alive, death is swallowed up in victory!

Prayer:

Lord, I thank you for dying on the cross for me. You paid the price for my sin. Help me today to walk in your righteousness and to tell others that you are Lord. Amen!

Day Twenty-Six

Alleluia, We Got a Savior

Scripture Reading Isa. 9: 1-7
Key Verse Isa. 9:6

"For unto us a child is born, unto us a son is given: and the government shall be upon his shoulder: and his name shall be called Wonderful, Counsellor, The mighty God, The everlasting Father, The Prince of Peace."

The key to a child born into a family is one of joy and celebration. Once it is found out that a child is conceive there are plans put in place followed by great expectation. To a great extent, there is also some levels of curiosity towards the gender maybe as a mean to determine what special gifts and name to select. The prophet Isaiah had prophesied the birth of the most awaited Messiah. Isaiah even went further describing some of the many roles and responsibilities of this special child. Most importantly this child would be a son! He would be over government and there are great and mighty significance to His name. Isaiah said His name shall be called IMMANUEL, interpreted "God with us." A divine person born to us as a son, how very unique? His name shall be called, Wonderful, His name here implies, wonder, marvelous things will happen from this son, things that are too high to articulate in the natural mind! He's the Counselor, to resolve, to deliberate, to guide, to devise. In fact, you can consult Him because he is the greatest advisor. A know all things advisor! He is the Mighty God, you cannot get anything bigger than that, He's Mighty! So mighty in battle, mighty to the pulling down of strongholds! Almighty! The Everlasting Father, this son will rule and reign forever, from everlasting to everlasting, there will be no end to His government! Of His throne there shall be no end!

Forever you can consult with Him and forever you'll see the demonstration of His power. The Prince of Peace, He will be the complete head, the Chief, the Captain forever! This son, God hath highly exalted Him and given Him a name that is above every name, that at the Name of Jesus every knee shall bow and every tongue shall confess that Jesus Christ is Lord! As you look and seek the direction of this our Savior, let's understand that this Lord and this Savior, is truly the best friend to have. Alleluia!

Prayer:

God, we rejoice in the fact that we have a Savior, your blessed Son Jesus Christ. We bless you and worship you, and we honor you today. Amen!

Day Twenty-Seven

A Settled Peace Beyond Measure

Scripture Reading John 14: 26- 31
Key Verse John 14: 27

"Peace I leave with you, my peace I give unto you: not as the world giveth, give I unto you. Let not your heart be troubled, neither let it be afraid."

When we consider the importance of the word of God and the comforts it gives, we realizes that His Word is much more than words on paper, His Words in fact are "WORDS OF LIFE", something we can consider to an extent, "LARGER THAN LIFE!" His words are bigger and better to us and for us than we can ever imagine. Think about it, "Jesus is really my peace!" Oh yes, He said it, my peace I leave with you, my peace I give you. What peace can one find in the world, especially in today's world? Nothing but an empty promise, yet, the Lord Christ gives comfort and reassurance, let not your heart be troubled, neither let it be afraid! What an amazement! Jesus is life, the Word is life! He, the giver of peace, one that passes all human understanding. Jesus told His disciples, it is expedient that I go, because if I go I will send you the comforter, I will send you the Holy Ghost! This Holy Ghost will be your guiding light, He will be the compass that you need, He will be the shade and the very peace to sustain you in the midst of great storms, something the world cannot give, and you can never put this on "lay away!" This is why it is so important that we dispatch to all that we encounter a taste of this peace that we receive from God, then the world will become a much better place. Christ the blessed hope of Glory, dwelling on the inside, you reflects even that same peace on the outside! Will you be the agent of peace to your community today? Will you be willing to share God's peace to others? It is beautiful, it is rewarding, it is fulfilling. Now that you are blessed with this peace, you must live your life as though you are really a true disciple of Christ, demonstrating to others the abundant peace of the Lord. Encouraging others whose hearts are troubled, let not your heart be troubled, neither let it be afraid.

Prayer:

Lord, help me to be that instrument or your peace. Let me share the love to all, the love that was shed abroad in my heart. I want other to see you reflecting through me. Thanks for being my peace today. Amen!

Day Twenty-Eight

Is There Something Wrong With Me?

Scripture Reading Gen. 6: 1-8
Key Verse Gen. 6: 6

"And it repented the Lord that he had made man on the earth, and it grieved him at his heart."

When God created man as we read in the book of Genesis, it was a beautiful plan for us to live healthy and righteous life here on earth. Man refuses to follow God's law and in disobedience sin came into our lives as a result. As in the case of Adam and Eve in the Garden of Eden the first family fell into sin by refusing to listen to God's instructions. Man was sinning in such a way, which actually grieved God. Today though, we have our Lord Jesus, which regardless of our abundant sin, He has provided grace and pardon to us. We are now able to live our lives in order to please God because grace is provided for us! Are we tired of this attitude bringing shame and dishonor to God our maker? The Bible says, there's a way that seems right unto a man but at the end, it leads to death. There are many of our actions that will ultimately lead to death and destruction. We no longer should conduct ourselves in ways that Will lead to death, ways which disobey and dishonor the Lord but to live and trusting in God's grace and his ability to forgive, in that God can relent and instead of Him been angry and grieved at our actions, He will show mercy. May God help us today to change the course of our lives and let us see Him moving and working strong on our behalf.

Prayer:

Father, I am sorry for my often rebellion and my negative attitude dishonoring you. Many times I get real stubborn and out of control with my behavior, yet I come to you. I trample on and at times abuse your grace. Lord am sorry, help me to live for you. Amen!

Day Twenty-Nine

A Life Honored By God

Scripture Reading Proverbs 15: 1-9
Key Verse Proverbs 14:34

"Righteousness exalteth a nation: but sin is a reproach to any people."

The Nation and the world overtime, had drifted from its core values and principles. God is expecting that we honor Him and abide by His words that we can effectively lead His people. We've seen overtime the severe damage caused by unrighteous governing. Leaders are to learn to lead in righteousness. Solomon new this well because he knew of his incapability's, and understood that he got some short comings, thus he asked God for wisdom. Solomon said, wisdom is a principle thing! There is something special about one that operate in the wisdom and fear of God. Solomon new that in order to prosper and successfully lead as God intends, he need the wisdom of God and not the way he see things. It is true that one will be exalted when he operate and conducts business in righteousness. The minute one fail to act righteously he's doomed. Solomon said it best, sin is a reproach to any people, in private practices, as public servant, wisdom of God is the way to acquire success. You can never prosper when taking sins approach, because God will not dwell in the tents of the Wicked, a life honored by God is one operated in righteousness.

Prayer:

Father please show us how to govern our family in righteousness, we understand that the only way we can prosper, help us we pray Amen!

Day Thirty

Nothing Matters Like Jesus

Scripture Reading Proverbs 14:1-13
Key verse Proverbs 14:13

"Even in laughter the heart is sorrowful; and the end of that mirth is heaviness."

It's amazing that one can be laughing, seem to be having fun yet deep down he is wounded, hurting and filled with grief and sorrow. Today, looking around us, there is too much hurts and pains in this dreaded economic upheaval. Beloved, this financial crisis is taking a serious toll on countless souls and instead of a smile, many have a frown. We realize that nothing brings me satisfaction like Jesus. There is an emptiness a void which can only be filled with a touch from the Lord. Once we relinquish all our cares and situations to Him, we can turn them into laughter again because He is still the greatest problem solver known to man! Yes, God understand the pain you are feeling today. Even in very difficult conditions when things seem hopeless and loss, Christ can make a difference if you will trust Him with your life. Yes those tears He will wipe away, you don't have to be cast down due to your unpaid bills, trust in God and you'll certainly be on your road to laughing again.

Prayer:

Oh God, you know it hurts real bad, we can't even talk about it too much we bring our life and conditions to you, do for us a miracle today. Amen.

www.ingramcontent.com/pod-product-compliance
Lightning Source LLC
LaVergne TN
LVHW051826080426
835512LV00018B/2735